Apocalyptic Witchcraft

PETER GREY

Apocalyptic Witchcraft

SCARLET IMPRINT

VERNAL EQUINOX · MMXIII

Published by Scarlet Imprint in 2013
under the *Bibliothèque Rouge* banner

© Peter Grey, 2013
Typography *&* design
by Alkistis Dimech

ISBN 978-0-9574492-9-9

Printed and bound in the United Kingdom.

SCARLETIMPRINT.COM

Images

I was a princess and thou didst scorn me. I was a virgin and thou didst take my virginity from me. I was chaste, and thou didst fill my veins with fire ... Ah! ah! Wherefore didst thou not look at me? If thou hadst looked at me thou hadst loved me. Well I know that thou wouldst have loved me, and the mystery of Love is greater than the mystery of Death.

Salomé

Exordium

Apocalyptic Witchcraft is written in the twilight of an age. It is a book which dares to prophesy. It is a new vision of an old way, but does no violence to tradition, treading as it does the paths of ancestry. This is an infusion of energy and movement. It is a witchcraft for those who know that the wheel of the year has broken from the spokes of the seasons. It does not ask for belief, adherence or followers. This is my parrhesia, and it simply asks that you listen.

This is a perilous book, and one which does not aim to please. We need neither the permission of god, nor man for what we do. Witchcraft casts its glamour through these pages, but it will not be prettified. The sickle moon cuts. The curse harms. The wound bleeds. Without these there is no life in witchcraft. Not all is baleful; we celebrate the healing growth, the joy of existence, and the matchless ecstasies of the sabbat whose tarnished meaning is patiently revealed. It is a lunar mystery, a woman's secret, kept by the very devil himself.

This is not a how-to book, or a compendium of folk remedies, nor is it a list of rituals for you to follow, nor strictly history. These have their place, yet my aim is stranger. I am not another would-be king of the witches. I give myself no titles. This is a naked proposition put before you; to read again the truths that give meaning to all these things. To ask, what is it that underlies the pattern of our magic? What is the essence of witchcraft itself?

Neither is this an easy book, though the ideas are simple enough, and they need to be expressed in the language of magic, as poetry. We must not forget that poets are at the sharp and bloody end of struggle. I will name the poets whose work lies behind my approach: Robert Graves, Peter Redgrove and Penelope Shuttle, and Ted Hughes. You may not know all their names or works. No matter, this is not a book about poetry – a marginalised art in its own right – but a book about witchcraft. These writers dared to confront the body of the witch, and from their work, and those they have inspired (notably Chris Knight) I have been able to draw the entire mythic landscape into sharp relief. This is no small claim. I have found a meaning and a myth which has the power to reignite witchcraft, a mythic structure which does not ask to overturn adherence to any given path, or violate any vows, but can send the fire surging through all of our limbs. Ultimately this dangerous thesis counsels unity and brokers a truce. For that reason, some will choose to reject it out of hand.

I have avoided archaic sounding language, ermine-trimmed as it often is with unfounded claims. My path is narrow and speaks directly to the heart. This can be frightening for those who confuse style with substance. I hope that this work demonstrates both, as I frankly acknowledge my sources, crediting the academics, anthropologists and archaeologists who lend their rigour and discipline to my argument, and the writers, artists and poets whose augury is sought when the doves and crows take flight, as they must. I have provided a select bibliography for further research, eschewing footnotes as I find that they break the flow of the text. I have the freedom to write more polemically than if I was imprisoned in the ivory tower of the academy, but do not have their resources. If I have taken liberties with ideas, then the mistakes are mine. If my writing is more ragged on the wing than the writers who precede me, I answer that it can still fly. If this work is needful of more time, I confess it is a luxury none of us possess. My wish is that readers find new avenues of inspiration from these sources, and enrich their practice with them. Time is of the essence now.

In my undertaking I have chosen words carefully. Not as a surgeon who arrays his instrument to dissect a cadaver under unblinking light, but as a thief who works in the dark. This work needs skilful fingers and quick wits. It is, as Jean Genet insists, a lover's art. My tools are those of instinct and of craft, honed by observation and application. Some may appear curious at first sight, but like the fine-lock'd words of the troubadours they are fashioned for a purpose. Understand that this is not like any book on witchcraft you have ever read before. I hope that it is all the better for it. So I make this request of the reader: follow the order of the book, as it is designed to open in a particular fashion. There is a peculiar logic at play. I have knelt at the threshold of this slim-waisted Judas gate, this hourglass filled with night, and found a way through the void between evening and morning star. Or perhaps, as is often the case with this work, I have been compelled, drawn through in spite of myself, listening to the sub-audial whisper of my Mistress who wants the door to yield. I do not present this book as a key, for keys contain no art. At best I have left the door to the labyrinth ajar.

My lineage is simple enough, it is revealed as the record of my work. My pen is a spear, thrusting after dreams. This is not a sequel to *The Red Goddess* – it is better considered as its secret heart. I have walked further now; my understanding has deepened and become all the more potent for it. Whereas I sought to destroy the exclusive and excluding language of magic in that book, this one is a more literary undertaking. There is a poem within this work too, a series of ten hymns to Inanna, for reasons that will become apparent, and for other reasons still hidden to me. I did not expect the answer which I would receive when I sought the goddess of witchcraft. The task was given to me. Apocalyptic witchcraft is the revealing, the uncovering of woman and the subject of Salomé's famous dance. Such an act has consequences for both the dancer and those who would watch but not partake.

You will recognise that I have written of the goddess who slakes herself on semen and blood. She who proclaims herself Finis, that this is the end. She who is the lust, the urge, the hunger, the most heightened state of life, and death. Like the opposer, she lures, she seduces, she lies, and ultimately kills; but not without purpose. Witchcraft is not a disjointed set of actions, but has meaning, substance, flesh.

Like the soul, this book has coagulated from menstrual blood. My argument hunts from the caves of our prehistory, through the fertile crescent, clots in the incubation chamber of Patmos, births as a nightmare in Europe and dreams itself into an apotheosis on the sabbat mount. It challenges us to be the witchcraft of our own time, for us to gain control of dreaming, of our lost land, of the body. It gives us back the broken myth in a form of devastating beauty and renewed relevance.

This work comes out of the lasting friendship of those in a wide variety of witchcraft and magical traditions who have supported my work, and that of Scarlet Imprint. Discretion counsels that they remain un-named. Here I will name only Alkistis, whose ideas permeate this shared work, the beloved whom I thought would never be found. Without her, not one word of this exists. I would also like to thank the Friends of the Museum of Witchcraft in Boscastle who allowed me to present the first draft of my sabbat thesis to them, and to our readers who attended *A Pleasure Dome* where the founding essay of this collection was inaugurated. Lastly, I should not forget to thank the doves and crows, for the conversations they have shared with me. It has been a long journey back to this beginning.

We start now with cymbals and end with thunder. The plough halts, stubborn in the furrow, above the storm turns as a mill wheel which no devil can arrest.

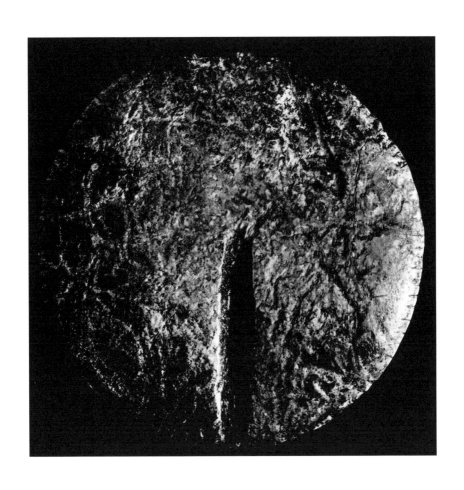

Inanna ascends
Adore her
Sweat stuck glitter
At the throat of evening
Flared staring eyes
Of moon's first daughter
Sing torch songs
For the stricken risen
Searchlight girl
Hoisted swelling
Forced from corsetry
Of underworld
A whore reborn

Apocalyptic witchcraft

How long can the moment stretch before climax? The vertiginous brink of consummation. Locks in the complex of concentric gates. Cryptographic tumblers meshed wet with the attar of roses. Exhortations spent. A hesitation held in the face of inexorable conquest. An intake of breath that must, finally, overcome, resisting, to the end, exhale. Transformed the raw plasma of storm pours from the dragon's mouth. The shockwave pulses out with the geometric driven precision of the heart beat after beat, after beat. It has begun. This atomic force, this raw force is Babalon. The storm breaks like a dropped glass whose shivering bell glimmers into infinity. The note remains ever distilling the same pitch. In the sabbat it resounds becoming a quiver of cymbals as strike bears down incessantly met by rising counterstrike. This is the sound the dancer makes when she moves. The bells at wrists, ankles, hips, earrings, shaking. The noise of battle reverberates through the armour in the deep secret cavities of our bodies. Here amongst the threshing limbs, the slaughter, she walks.

This is the emblem of the unfolding of the rose amongst the flames. A million orgasms intersecting their petals through all space and time. A message comes through to those who would be present at such a sabbat: *Get rid of yourself.*

But this endless moment, the bacchanal can lead us away from the most salient fact of witchcraft. Though, as Jack Parsons says, witchcraft is the oldest religion, that it lifts us out of ourselves and switches our bristling skin, the fact is that witchcraft arises from the world. It comes from the land, the people, the plants, the animals, the whole web of life. Do not let anyone tell you otherwise. Witchcraft is here in present time.

When I say apocalyptic witchcraft it is deliberately antagonistic because I see witchcraft being used as an excuse for solipsistic escapism when it is the exact opposite. I situate witchcraft in the world as it is. As radical changes cascade through the living systems of the biosphere, tradition must by necessity change. This fluid transformation is the beauty and strength that marks true craft. As such it will upset those who cling to form. So be it. There is not simply tradition, there is innovation there is becoming and there is revolution. This is a woman's truth, this is the goddess who has spun through history to be with us now.

Witchcraft has a history of remembering its radical heritage whether through Michelet, Jack Parsons or feminism, and also of inventing itself anew. Montague Summers writes: 'Witches, satanists and the whole unhallowed crew were meddling with and mixing in politics from the first, and as their liege lord, the Devil, rebelled against God in heaven, so do they rebel against any ordered and legitimate form of government on earth.'

I say that it is on the cusp of doing so again, and with good reason. Though the sabbat itself arguably only dates from 1650, it connects to a far older tradition of nocturnal gatherings on the high places born from both celebration, and in response to attacks on the people, as well as a demonisation of such assemblies both to protect them from prying eyes and to criminalise the participants. It is in this renewal, and not the faux old or the endless inquisition into what is traditional, where witchcraft is to be found.

The bald heath has witnessed the dance of the atom turn volteface. The splitting of the light in an apocalypse that we have wrought. World's end is not a threat from the pulpit, we have assembled it with dextrous and sinistrous fingers, bunkered our oblivion for the days of the final division of plunder now at hand. We will not follow the smoke to the stars until we are burned on the pyre of the earth. Love is the war to end all wars, and the war is upon us.

While our culture laments, what have we done wrong? Has no concept of sin, but only consumption. It still knows that something is going dreadfully awry. Infantilised it helplessly repeats, what, what have we done wrong?

It is simple: Mankind has broken the covenant with nature.

Dee and the alchemists knew this, and sought to coax from their alembics a gentler reconciliation, an harmonious counterchange of the elements cross-matched. That window has closed. There is no gold that will buy us freedom from our fate, we are more fearsomely tasked. As our vaunted technological sophistication hits built-in obsolescence it is the deceptively simple acts and tools of witchcraft that will endure. I would trust my black-handled knife longer than my laptop. If more high magicians had, like Paracelsus, listened to the folk practitioners rather than their vanity we would perhaps not be at this point. Yet we are.

We must recognise that we are the horsemen that sheet upon the winds. We the angels pouring poison vials. We the seal breakers. We the elders of days revolving around an empty throne. We the daughters of Jerusalem, the Kings of Edom, the Cains and Liliths, the scorpion men. Before we turn our deserving ire on the class of the super-rich and their marauding corporations we must recognise that we too are the consumers. Our actions have added to the weight of disenchantment. We have let this happen.

The rape of the earth is about to enter a horrifying final phase where the last wildernesses are despoiled for the last resources.

Should we weep? The words of Medea, daughter of the Sun and priestess of the witch-goddess Hekate, can be considered here, as an inspiration from the sharp pen of Seneca. Whilst her Nurse pleads caution, Medea responds as sorceress:

MEDEA: Light is the grief which can take counsel and hide itself; great ills lie not in hiding. 'Tis pleasing to face the foe.
NURSE: Stay this frenzied outburst my child; even silent calm can scarce defend thee.
MEDEA: Fortune fears the brave, the cowardly overwhelms.
NURSE: No hope points out a way for our broken fortunes.
MEDEA: Whoso has naught to hope, let him despair of naught.
NURSE: The Colchians are no longer on thy side, thy husband's vows have failed, and there is nothing left of all thy wealth.
MEDEA: Medea is left – in her thou beholdest sea and land, and sword and fire and gods and thunderbolts.

Such is our state. Such is the goddess of witchcraft and the figure of the witch in the line of Medea. There is no escape. Witchcraft is already dead as a hag, as barren as the moon, as contaminated as the tar sands. Yet witchcraft is born again in this sacred despoiled landscape, and will be despised as an abomination by those who cannot navigate by the candlelight of guttering stars. Those who seek to escape the fates and furies will learn that they are inexorable. We celebrate this, wreathed in the afterglow with a half-life of a million million years. We the murderers, the poisoners, the tightening noose of curse, the fire on the mountain.

We have a reply to this savaged world, a confession that need not be racked out of us: It is we who have drunk from the cup. We who are drunk on the blood of sacrifice. We who flower from our wounds. We who celebrate Love and War. We who know mystery. We are the Witchcraft.

Witchcraft does not wait for deliverance. It kisses and kills with the same flushed bloody mouth. We cannot bridle her utterance, the whore speaks. We are not separate from the fate of the world. We are used to being unwelcome, hunted, blamed, raped, tortured, dispossessed, disappeared. Now we are an irrelevance, a harmless eccentricity, a fairy ball sporting stick on ears and dressing up box deviance, a social joke. Yet as witchcraft is filled with the spirit of the age we will become dangerous again, because witchcraft will have rooted meaning.

Apocalypse is not escapism, as some suggest. It is being held in the jaws at the threshold of life and death. It is sacred confrontation and revelation. It is utopia and dystopia in eternal exchange. It sees through. In Christianity, apocalypse is used by the world haters who argue for war, in the New Age as a panacea for those who long for ascension; I use it to awaken us from dream.

There is no other way to talk about apocalypse. I do not choke the inspiration in my throat. I will not simply watch the last dance or describe the dancers without losing myself amongst them. We must be brought to an awareness of the moment.

We have the power to destroy the world and we are doing so. Witchcraft must respond as it always has, to the events which unfold around us with the gifts we have been given and those which we have won on the heath. Having entered into the moment, we can go back, but not a moment sooner. So we ask the looking glass our question, what is witchcraft?

In the search for origins we ask who we are. Not a miasma of deception to drape over the show stone, rather a blood thread that spins into a mantle, a living web of connection.

What is witchcraft?

The answer is simple: witchcraft is the work of the enemy. Witchcraft is the sex that other people have, witchcraft the drug that other people take, witchcraft is the rite that other people perform. Witchcraft is the magic that other people do. Witchcraft is the clothes that other people wear. Witchcraft is the words that other people speak. Witchcraft the goddess they venerate.

It is impossible to reach any other conclusion. For the whole of recorded history witchcraft has been malefica, venefica, incest and murder. The next village, the next town, the next country, the old woman, the young woman, the Jew, the leper, the Cathar, the Templar, the Ophite, the Bogomil. They do it. Not us you understand, them. You will find the witch at the end of a pointed finger.

To argue otherwise is a fatal mistake that opens us to divide and conquer. To prettify witchcraft is as ill-judged as to disfigure it. You cannot deny the goddess in any form of cast lantern light or play of shadows. You cannot say white witchcraft or black witchcraft without doing violence to her complete being. It is time that we heal this wound. Consider the words of the Thunder Perfect Mind: *I am the whore and the holy one.*

So let us explore our definition with the aid of a book that means so much to us. The *Malleus Maleficarum* in defining witchcraft identifies three vital components: The witch, the devil, and the will of God. The witch, as we have seen, is the other, the foreigner and, more often than not, the woman. The devil is the double, whose worship is nocturnal, orgiastic and child-killing. The will of God is the power of the Church and State to oppress, to accuse, and to enact the auto-da-fé.

An apocalyptic witchcraft will contain these self-same elements: the witch, as foreign woman, exemplified by Inanna-Ishtar and demonised in the Bible as the Whore of Babylon. As populations are displaced by war, flood, fire and famine, we will see many more strangers in a strange land. To the witch, they are kindred.

The devil as the mask of wild nature and the goddess, giving us the choice to control our bodies, minds and destiny. We have already seen Baphomet as a cipher for Mohammed, and Islam will not be the only bedevilled enemy. Ecologists, feminists, psychonauts, shamans, will continue to be decried in these terms. But just as Tupac Shakur confronted the American psyche as the n— thug and drew strength from it, turned the nightmare back on them, so we can choose to embrace the devil that they deny.

The will of God is a clear understanding of, and opposition to, the designs of our enemy. This does not mean simply destroying the mythic structure of the Christian Church, which gave man nature to despoil, just the cedars of Lebanon were cut down for Yahweh, but the final ugly phase of this ideology: corporatist fascism. We are the final line of resistance.

But what of modern pagan witchcraft? Why has it not risen to these challenges? The difficulty with modern pagan witchcraft is that it began with compromise. Gardner had one eye on the recent repeal of the witchcraft laws. 'And it harm none' was rather more expedient than the hair-raising pronouncements of Cecil Williamson or the misanthropy of Spare. Yet it is foolish to simply attack Gardner or Sanders or Cochrane or Graves. They were responding to the spirit of their age. It seemed for an impossible heady moment that witchcraft was going to become the new religion of England. That project is in disarray.

Now Ronald Hutton says not simply harm none, but be harmless. Having seen the Nigerian witch killers and the Satanic Panic of the eighties, he argues that we are better off to live in a disenchanted world and escape on the weekends to our imaginal worlds of whimsical delight.

I say, fear us.

I say that the power of the witch is in having every option open. Witchcraft will not lie beneath, will not be disarmed. Women know this. We do not want to be inside, having interfaith meetings with the hand-wringing monotheists whose holy books sanction our stoning, murder and rape.

Witchcraft, and by that I mean malefica, is the strong face we show to this world. This is the merciless path.

A good witchcraft example of this is the solonaceae, the family which includes mandrake and datura. Solonaceae comes from the root *solari*, to soothe; indeed, these daughters of comfort both cure and kill. They enable us to fight poison with poison. There is no way to separate the powers and no way we should be cleaved from our rights to exercise either.

So is there an alternative narrative to that of Gardner? One approach is that of traditional craft. Paul Huson neatly explains the difference when he says:

Traditional witchcraft is what Margaret Murray – a British historian who during the twenties advanced the notion that Witchcraft was originally a clandestine pagan religion that had continued to exist alongside Christianity – referred to as 'Operative Witchcraft,' to distinguish it from what she called 'Ritual Witchcraft.' Operative Witchcraft, to use her words, encompassed all charms and spells, whether used by a professed witch or by a professed Christian, whether intended for good or for evil, for killing or for curing. Ritual Witchcraft, on the other hand, embraced the religious beliefs and ritual of those who practiced what Murray referred to as the Dianic Cult, the worship of a deity that was incarnate in a man, a woman, or an animal, traces of which she believed were to be found in Italy, in Southern France, and in the English Midlands. The god was named Janus or Dianus, the goddess Diana. 'Wicca' or 'Wica' was arguably G.B. Gardner's own personal take on the Dianic cult.

Huson's *Mastering Witchcraft* is a key text of traditional Craft, but Huson clearly states that he drew on the same material as Gardner from the folklore library at University College London. Plainly stated, they both cut it from the same cloth. It is fair to say that traditional craft, though containing earlier and folkloric elements, is as invented as Gardnerian Wicca, and by that I mean no disrespect to either.

Yet now we see the manufacturing of a schism between a supposed traditional craft and initiated Wicca. It is an attempt to separate the inseparable and rewrite a history of shared protagonists, as the example of The Regency demonstrates, and on an island of widely diverse practice that cannot be neatly embroidered into one gypsy myth. The new strands of 'old' witchcraft show where Wicca was remiss, namely plant lore, low magic and folklore. But to define oneself in opposition to your closest allies in a battle of authenticity seems fatally flawed, especially when most of our history is chronicled by our enemies and further spans the shifting landscapes of literature, poetry, vision and dream.

Furthermore, how is a Cain-Lilith myth any different or more valid than a Diana-Lucifer one? Who exactly enforces that Wiccans do no operative magic, or ensures traditional crafters have no religious or mythic underpinning? In fact what we see now is a supposedly traditional craft enthusiastically fashioning exactly the kind of ritual witchcraft that they have decried the Gardnerians for. The reason is that they are part of a divided whole which is not simply true of witchcraft, but our entire culture's schism and denial of the complete goddess whom we dare to know incarnate as Babalon.

This horizontal hostility between people who should share the same interests is exactly the tactic employed by COINTELPRO. It splinters, it dissipates, it prevents us engaging with the real enemy. There are more pressing issues than whether we work naked or robed. Enough. I say, my enemy's enemy is my friend. When I say apocalyptic witchcraft I also mean the destruction of the false differences between the traditions.

Gerald Gardner's witchcraft was not ultimately about the form, it was about the force. A culture crawling out of the bombed cellars of London into the new world of pill and possibility. The witchcraft of Jack Parsons was not about the form, it was about the force of the bohemian sexual revolution and entheogenic drugs. Traditional witchcraft is not about the form, it is about the harrowing loss of folklore, rural life and, crucially, meaning in a postmodern world.

Apocalyptic witchcraft is about a world at war with the last remnants of wild nature, the last remnants of humanity, and so I am here concentrating on conjuring that force rather than entering into the trap of circumscribing it. Those who have read *The Red Goddess* will know that I am adamantly opposed to the imposition of orthodoxy. So when I say apocalyptic witchcraft I am describing a set of ideas that can be embodied in any witchcraft approach. We should celebrate every form of emergent heresy. Our emails are, after all, read by the same intelligence agencies. Our ritual sites photographed by the same military satellites. Our wells poisoned by the same fertilisers, fracking and pharmaceuticals.

We must never forget our enemy. However peaceable we believe we are, they define us with violence. Witchcraft was born in the torture chambers of the inquisition. Unclothed, bound, broken, taught to fly in strappado.thinder per

In the 1200s the enemy was the Cathars who threatened the Catholic Church by espousing poverty. In the 1300s the enemy was heresy, exemplified in the destruction of the Templars. In the 1400s it became the figure of the witch that subsequently blossomed into an international satanic conspiracy. Why did this happen? Why did the sabbat obtain such prominence? Why did the witch become so reviled? Without understanding the enemy there is no answer that can be given.

The creation of a purely malefic figure of the witch was an attack on women, though men too were burned. Woman was attacked in this way to enable the state to enclose the common land. Woman was attacked to remove her control over her womb. Woman was attacked to divide the sexes and rend the social fabric. Woman was attacked to destroy the sense of the sacred in nature. Woman was memory of ancestor and clan.

We do not need to follow Marx, we need simply to follow the money. The process has continued because the enemy has inexhaustible greed and diminishing returns. It is not simply the commons that are enclosed, everything is being sold into the hands of the few. This means war, and the war is upon us.

The sabbat arose as a conspiracy to destroy the rotten edifice of Church and State, meeting on the heath to avoid the gaze of the authority, guised in anonymity and foreboding. This revolutionised the nature of witchcraft, regardless of the pre-existence of the sabbat form. I do not simply refer here to the inspiring fantasies of Jules Michelet, but the important modern work of Silvia Federici.

We see the same attacks on freedom of assembly in the destruction of the free festivals, rave culture and the occupy movement. These have been met by the masked Anonymous, the faceless black bloc anarchists, the direct actions of the ELF. These are expressions of popular witchcraft and have been persecuted by the same inquisition that came for us. I do not say that these are examples of operative witchcraft, I say that we, the people who are the witchcraft, have a sacred duty to join this war. We need to celebrate Grand Sabbats again, infuse them with our witchblood, our cunning.

Here is my prophecy. Witchcraft is going to get both aroused and angrier. Nature will rise. We are not only coming for your children, we are your children and all those who will inherit the ruins of the world. Welcome to the apocalypse. This is the moment when we realise that the climate is broken. It's all blood and roses from here on in. As witches we should prepare to fly on the wings of the storm.

This is War
The gods await judgement
Cuffed and kneecapped
Cowed
Sliver cradles killer star
The vision given
New moon blood
Washed from cut
Falls on earth as rain

A manifesto of apocalyptic witchcraft

1   If the land is poisoned then witchcraft must respond.

2   It is not our way of life, it is life itself which is under threat.

3   Witchcraft is our intimate connection to the web of life.

4   We are the Witchcraft.

5   Our world has forever changed.
The trodden paths no longer correspond.
Witchcraft thrives in this liminal, lunar, trackless realm.

6   We are storm, fire and flood.

7   We will not be denied.

8   Witchcraft is the recourse of the dispossessed, the powerless, the hungry and the abused. It gives heart and tongue to stones and trees. It wears the rough skin of beasts. It turns on a civilisation that knows the price of everything and the value of nothing.

9   If you have no price you cannot be bought.
     If you do not want you cannot be bribed.
     If you are not frightened you cannot be controlled.

10   Witchcraft is folk magic, the magic of the people and for
     the people.

11   We call an end to the pretence of respectability.

12   We will not disarm ourselves.

13   The War is upon us.

14   Choose then to become a Mask.

15   Those with nothing left to lose will dare all.

16   There is one witchcraft under many names.
     There is one grand sabbat on one mountain.
     There are many ways to fly.
     There is no witness present at the sabbat.

17   Witchcraft is a force, not an order.
     Witchcraft is rhizomatic, not hierarchic.
     Witchcraft defies organisation, not meaning.
     We simply bear the marks.

18   Witchcraft is power and possesses this in ekstasis, sex
     and ordeal.

19   Witchcraft is unbridled sexuality.
     In witchcraft it is the woman who initiates.
     We challenge man to be the equal of this woman.

20 Witchcraft is the art of inversion.

21 Witchcraft is the beauty which is terror.

22 Witchcraft is a myth, which drawing on the past, clothes
   itself in the symbols of (its) time.
   Witchcraft does not mistake myths for history, it harnesses
   them to transform the future.
   Witchcraft knows the ground upon which it stands.

23 Witchcraft honours the spirits.
   Witchcraft enchants for the lost.
   Witchcraft will not forget.

24 Witchcraft embodies our ancestors and saints, they carry us
   with them.

25 To Her is offered the blood, to us the care of the ash and
   bones.

26 The example we follow is our own.

27 The practice of witchcraft is one of revolution and of the
   power of woman.

28 The goddess who speaks through us is known among men
   as Babalon.

29 Witchcraft concerns itself with mystery.
   Through the gates of mystery we come to knowledge.
   Knowledge enters us through the body.
   The highest form of this knowledge is Love.

30   Every drop of blood is sacrificed to the grail.
      Love cannot be bought with any other coin.

31   We seek and drink this wine together.

32   Will is finite, passion infinitely renewed.

33   Witchcraft is present, it is ensanguined and vivified.
      Witchcraft is prescient, it gazes on the future.
      Witchcraft is oracular, it will not hold its tongue.
      Our time has come.

III

Who sings this?
Hymns our lady?
Coin clinks finger cymbals?
Drums up the storm?
Bitch queens leathermen
Sapphic catastrophes
Come forth
Come out
Come armed
In holy Inanna's name
Supernova bloom
In bowel and sex and throat
On breast and back and palms
She is here
In hot thrust of spear
In endless violation

She is without

The cats have seen us. Belly-slunk hunters of the ravines which thunder winter storms into the waiting bay. Lizards thrashing off warm rocks into the waiting rue flee from our footsteps. Fennel, clover and bee orchids, nightshades and thorns are watched over by silver-backed ravens. Pine trees stand clung with the spume of insect spittle. We are the only pilgrims on this unsigned path, and pilgrims must walk barefoot when possible and absorb the messages left for them by history.

Eucalyptus, another alien invader, poisons the water and with flickering leaves distracts from the groans of the resinous trees. So we got out our pocket knife and carved our names into one. Just beneath a cleft with a smooth warm furrow like my lover's sex. Cut in the angular Greek script and stripped away a heart. It will still be there, down from the well where we uncovered a hymen spider's web spun patiently above the black water. A secret under rough stone and rusted grate. But all this is without.

The cave is hidden now, beneath a whitewash spiral of steps built on the living chthonic rock. Beneath a ramshackle church thrown over it. Beneath a moon that pours her upturned cup onto it from a perfect blue sky.

Miraculous, a rose bush twines up from the monastic garden and offers us flowers. We can scarcely believe that we are here. That the

cave is unguarded against us. World Heritage signs are leaned care-
lessly here and there, as if the sleepy island also cannot believe that
Christendom would care for this alcove on their few square miles of
broken stones and bays. And largely, it does not. The clinging diesel
nausea of a night ferry from Piraeus has cleared. An Athens of riot
scars far behind.

The door is barred, so we sun ourselves on the bedrock and sight
the hills, the outcrops, the sand spits, the distance. Pick bitters from
between the stones and test them with our teeth. Loll as lions on the
rocks as the monks go about whatever business it is they have when
a world has lost their orthodoxy behind four foot thick white walls.
From the first foray we return with a rose and at the harbour square
drink coffee, eat cake drenched in honey. We are two lovers on an
island empty of tourists who lurk offshore in belching cruise ship
prison pens troughing through buffets of safely non-Greek food and
await being herded through the briefest of landfalls by their liveried
shepherds. Our night on the island has unmediated stars and cica-
das. The voices of the dead in a static of carapace and bent legs.

Rising early we walk the path, wearing it to familiarity. Coaches
grind up the road, hidden from us. The cave will be open, as the
hand-painted sign said. They will not see us, do not expect us, the
pilgrims that John had dispatched into sulphur lakes and chain and
pinion by angelic host. We are the last people that would come back
here, eschatological escape artists, the enemy. We enter, still unno-
ticed, and descend a further staircase, before crossing the threshold
mosaic of a seven pointed star, into the cave of the Apocalypse of
John.

So it is here that John wedged himself into hiding. A seashell curl
of pitted ceiling, fissured floor. An ear festooned with the trinkets of
the orthodox. Lantern strings of silver and gaudy shades. Icons to be
kissed on the feet. Frankincense slights the cool air, the goat shit reek
of the past masked.

We light a candle to her. A silent prayer in a Nero's garden of vota-
ries. We trespass.

A cross is hewn into the wall. Rough triangular ends, like heaps of grain. He may have cut this, before the icon had become fixed, the withered Northern Sun god on spindling straws. Or perhaps Proclus cut it, or some later pilgrim. In this tomb he will have felt like the Christ, as cold, as dead, as blind; wondering when the exile would be over. A pleading of *tamata* where his pillow was. *Heal my eyes, my ears, my heart...* Requests the pagans would have found orthodox, and John would have disdained. His head sunk in a further rock shroud incubates only deeper nightmares.

Somehow John caught whispers amplified in this nautilus chamber. A conch shell trumpet which we now strain to hear. It fissures through his bones that feel lit by lightning.

What was this for him? Who was his Babylon? Can the now lead words be unrolled from the defixio, the limbs twisted back into comely shapes. Does our presence break the seal on the vessel.

A-line Christians, wan sickened troglodytes make the pilgrimage in ankle socks, by bus. An ill and subterranean race. Elbowing babooshkas accompany the latest generation of Rasputins still keeping it orthodox rocking over-sized gangster crosses and untrustworthy beards. Vomited bemused from cruise ships are the tourists, unsure of even the barest Bible verse but content to be herded around another attraction seen through a viewfinder. But these distractions pass, and day after day we have more time alone in the cave. A priest breaks inexplicably into song which probes the rock for resonance. We attend devoutly.

The island never finds him. Marigolds, poppy reds, proud purples open in a Spring which cannot unfurl in the cave. He feeds on bitter herbs, not honey. A Hades grown so hateful that the Persephone he drags down remains chaste, spat at with curse words. Against the Sybils and Pythia he fills his mouth not with laurel leaves, but thorns. In his bunker testament his struggling Greek preserves the heresy. His blind eyes are on Ephesus, on Rome, on Helena in her chamber. All priestesses who speak with the voice of the Earth he condemns to eternal Winter. No petals will open to the sun, unless tortured Christ returns to blight and blame. Ishtar is split into Maria and Whore, the wound is opened.

It is a dreaming war, become nightmare. John gabbles back the myths of the Titans stripped of star stuff and now garbed in the wolfish skins of Roma. Worms his hypnagogic cell into the resentful catacombs of the bishops' minds in Nicea. Turns his persecution into a resonant string of open-ended curses. The date, the numbers are uncertain and erased in a prophecy now set loose to devour in the garden.

Torch runners will have snaked past the cave mouth, just as we did, to Chora on the hill. But the temples fell to brooding black stone. A monstrous basalt eruption buried the white marble columns in a forbidding Christian ossuary. A treasure house to defy the Turkish pirates. A vice set over the island. An irrelevance on the tourist shop stop that punctuates the end of the island chain. An opportunity to sip another frappé. Still, a pair of doves at the monastery door await the return of Scythian Artemis, and clapped up heavenward at our approach.

There are few icons of Apocalypse in the monastery, a sword-tongued Jesus tucked down altar left with seven-faced candlesticks, seven angels bearing the churches of Asia Minor across the glittering sea. There is gospel John, not plague John, not fire John, not locust John. Wheeled and winged angels regard us with a baleful eye from the frescos. Know why we have come.

It is the Middle Ages when his Christ speaks, tongue red as the wet-dipped spear of Longinus. Pock marked and rose scarred with buboes: a pox on woman and man. The lamb's blood crosses fail to impede the heedless Angel of Black Death. The Jews suffer least, to the horror of the Church. Comets come, the hairy stars and crosses cannot deflect their baleful flight, their cruel influence on destiny.

The Nazarene remains resolutely nailed to his cross. Refuses to descend. Insists that we witness his torment some more. Taunts for a comeback he will never fulfil. Nature will act before he ever does.

We walk more of the island as John might have. Drop over the flank and skirt the Nunnery, which like the nuns is cowled, rounded backs and shoulders, closed to the world. Matins and Vespers, anticipating the orbital of pirates. A clattered rock sets an adder all a-hiss. We cool ourselves in the boulder rolling sea and drink the last of our water. Pad over dirt roads and quarries, roads bleached clear of markings. We catch glances of a bay that could be the sandspit of a beached abortive attempt to return to Turkey, a sea that vomited forth monsters. Yet it seems John will not have strayed far from his cave, looking down on the lee-side of the harbour, forever elsewhere, carried on his letters and a bitter miasma of corrupting dreams as his eyes gutter out.

Greeks have kept their ancient faces, drink retsina and fart around the square on mopeds in captain's hats as the priests amble round for kafedaki and karidopita. The men, apotropaic, touch their balls when the pillarbox and black hierophants have passed. Time slowly mends and unravels monofilament nets on the quayside.

For a week as lovers we are welcomed, jugs of retsina, sheep milk feta, steamed horta appears miraculous at our taverna table and the cost is waved away. Our room replenished with yet more roses. There are no other visitors staying on the island this early in the Spring. We search for more traces of John. There is a chapel at the murder site. Here the soft-mouthed mullet brought the shine back to Knopos' skull which the octopi concealed in the depths of a smashed amphora. Another glorious killing of a pagan saint who no longer tombstones from the rocky headlands. It is a wearily familiar tale.

It is sparce here, the bronze axes did their work all too well and the trees sailed away, followed by the topsoil. The fishing fleet does not have red blood in their gaping gills. Yachts nose in from Turkey, though not enough to make a difference. It is a world in the process of being forgotten. In the echo chamber of the cave we began a new song, though the world which John transformed has only the reckoning left.

Surveying our treasures on the bed, we have one just budded rose, boxed rocks of incense, church candles, dirt, the bare charm essentials. It is time to leave. Patmos is clothed in sun, open on all sides with bays and beaches, crowned nightly with stars, lit up. There is a final jug of wine and a night on the floor of a throbbing ferry with gypsies who when the Greeks rush for the Piraeus dawn caution their children, *let the fishes go*. From such an end can come only beginnings.

The cup, the cross
and the cave

The work of witchcraft is intimately connected with dreaming; some say it is simply that.

Yet it is a mistake to simply believe that dream is a landscape that is an untracked wilderness, that our visions are any more substantial than the gauzy projections of Prospero. We must ask what and who has created such bewitching visions for us. If we are rather stricken by narcolepsy than rapt in flight or set on somnambulistic tread to the sabbat then is dream itself being thieved, and the stagehands replacing the interior world with props, fashioned for another's art to be revealed nightly behind the moth wing fall of tiring eyes? Are the rare dreams we seek retreating down an endless corridor? Has Prospero such power over the denizens of his island? Can we predict that it is witchcraft that will find a trackless path through this all, return from exile once more? These are the mysteries of the cup the cross and the cave.

Dream, I will argue, is made. The metaphor that first needs to be grasped is one that bears repeating, that of a war on dreaming. The decisive action here is the one embarked upon by John of Patmos, another exile bound to a far flung isle. His was a deliberate action which set out not merely to loose chimeras in the garden of the mind, but to bar the gates of dream itself. So this is where we decant our vitriol and dissolve the locks that John applied, which state and

Church imposed. This is by no means the end of the process, but the point at which we choose to begin.

Revelation is a prismatic text, one which refracts whatever light you shine upon it and plays out its magic lantern show of fears and hopes and, dare I say it, dreams. What marks my exegesis is that I have trod in the footsteps of John, and literally tracked him to his lair. Without making pilgrimage we cannot fully understand. Dream can be considered another typology of this going forth, and one which characterises all forms of witchcraft. Dream was perhaps the only weapon left to John, seeing the fading hope of his cult and absent saviour. He was exiled to forgetfulness, and either blind or losing his sight crept deeper into the living rock and the companionship not only of Proclus but of memories and hopes and hatred.

But dream too was the weapon which he saw was wielded by his enemies, both in the God propaganda of Rome writing its stories in stone, pressing them onto coin, swathed in imperial purple and incense offerings, and the cult of the oracular priestess. The genius of John was to combine the hate figures in a scopolamine haze of limbs and deeds and accounts of the early church. His was a dream to end both empires, of Roma and Amor, of Caesar and Woman. Thus in Revelation we have woman at her most despised, as jewelled as any icon, as reviled as any hag, as desired as any whore. The witch is the final form of the despoiled goddess, her immortality, and ultimately the form in which she will enact her revenge.

The magical act of John was one of witchcraft: dreaming. We can be more specific and give it the ancient title: incubation. Incubation is a magical healing art that has been forgotten by our culture. Dream in the ancient world was something that happened, not mere imagination. Therefore the first step in this process of our reclamation is to place a high value upon dream, something this culture has denied. The private dream has been replaced with a public dream arena of popular symbols, an arena in which dream itself has been absented. The nightly adventure into sleep is not accorded value, and neither are any of our liminal states. To daydream is forbidden, to pursue visions psychosis. The permitted nether realm is only that which we share in visual mass culture. Our desires have been not only named, but branded.

The diving bell of psychoanalysis has been hauled to the surface, trespassing as it did in the world of magic, and dream has once more been marginalised and mocked as insubstantial. We need to lend it massy weight. Our conception of dreams needs healing before we can in turn be healed by them. There is no price which can be placed upon this.

The second step is to prevent leakage, be chaste in who we share our dreams with. The dreaming vessel is lost with all hands, swamped by the waves when exposed to those who are not ready to understand. Keep silent. The dream figure raises thumb and forefinger to lips in the gesture of the initiate of the mysteries. Our task is not to passively drop out, but to consciously disconnect. The dream diary is a practice to cultivate, or our dreams fall away forgotten. This connects us to a ritual continuum, as the one obligation of those cured through incubation was to write down their dream and leave it as a votive. We must learn to extend our control, not allow others to descend for us and peer out through thick glass, but plunge in ourselves as naked as pearl divers and return with the treasures of the undersea garden.

Incubation is to sleep in a sacred place, and seek out the healing dream. The incubation cult was spread throughout the Middle East and in Egypt, grouped about Serapis and Isis and Imhotep, whereas the Greek was concerned with mantic Asclepius the divine healer, and Apollo of the plague-bearing arrows. Asclepius with serpent, dog and gilded fingers is the guide who would rival Christ as a healer; he has as such been excised from the memory of history.

So we must after a sequence of chastity (which is not to be gained by crossing either ourselves or our legs) and bathing and purifying, seek out the sacred adytum. At the very least our bedchambers must be considered our sanctuaries, our temples, our secret hearts. This is where practice begins in earnest. We should also hunt our dreams, seek out and sleep in the places of wisdom, beneath thorn bushes, hedges, datura trees.

Those who returned to the cave were swaddled in the clothes of infants reinforcing the connection between cave, sleep, death and re-birth from the literal underworld. Initiation in dream is thus revealed as the birth rite of witchcraft. Our origin is embedded in the land of the dead and færy, concealed within the ringing hollow hills.

The dreamer would often embark upon the night sea journey, an image for an island dwelling race that we perhaps know better as the Sabbat flight. Often the cure would come in the form of a serpent, who had the gift of pharmakon, being both poison and remedy. Here the serpent was identified explicitly with the healer god Asclepius. The serpent would oil towards them, as surely as the anacondas of ayahuasca dreamscapes, gliding mouth wide. As the affirmation goes: *Poison is our nectar, poison is our grail, the wine of poison courses through our veins.* The serpent was an image of the ancestor and wisdom before it became vilified in Christianity, mainly due to its role in Genesis. This demonisation drastically severed us from the hero cult of our personal deified dead, a subject championed by Jake Stratton-Kent in his *Geosophia*. Worth also noting here is the serpent veneration in the Isis cult, another unwelcome competitor to the Christian story.

This serpent and dog of Asclepius are chthonic motifs. The dog is the psychopomp and guide to the underworld, as well as the eater of corpses. Both these necromantic animals are also given to Hek-ate, the howls of her dogs and wolves rending the veil between the worlds of living and dead. As Queen of the Night she is the send-er of nocturnal dreams, prophetic vision, ghosts and nightmares. She has the power to summon the dead to appear *in visu noctis*. The dreams of witchcraft now inhabit these dread margins.

Originally the dream was the cure in its entirety. The vision of the god enabled the deep healing to take effect. The votive tablets cached at Epidauros attest to the efficacy of the cure. This deep heal-ing has been clinically observed in the hypnotic state. Perhaps this second century account by Roman orator Ælius Aristides in his *Sacred*

Orations will help us begin to walk down the marble stairs polished by so many feet:

> The revelation was unquestionable, just as in a thousand other instances the epiphany of the god was felt with absolute certainty. You have a sense of contact with him, and are aware of his arrival in a state of mind intermediate between sleep and waking; you try to look up and are afraid to, lest before you see him he shall have vanished; you sharpen your ears and listen, half in dream and half awake; your hair stands up, tears of joy roll down, a proud kind of modesty fills your breast. How can anyone really describe this experience in words? If one belongs to the initiated, he will know about it and recognise it.

Here Aristides is clearly in the state of neither-neither. This liminality is the realm of myth, divinity, dream and the dead. Such a vision was not only given by a god, but was originally given by the great mother. Her earliest form must surely have been the cave bear, whose cult skulls were venerated in the caves of our ancestors. We need to go this deep to seek our vision of the goddess or devil, but let us for now cite Apuleius who, in his *Metamorphoses*, gives us the vision of Isis which he received:

> Scarcely had I closed my eyes, when lo, from the midst of the deep there arose that face divine to which even the gods must do reverence. Then a little at a time, slowly, her whole shining body emerged from the sea and came into full view. I would like to tell you all the wonder of this vision... First the tresses of her hair were long and thick, and streamed down around her softly, flowing and curling about her divine neck. On her head she wore as a crown many garlands of flowers, and in the middle of her forehead shone white and glowing a round disc like a mirror, or rather like the moon; on its right and left it was bound about with the furrowed coils of rising vipers, and above it were stalks of grain. Her tunic

was of many colours, woven of the finest linen, now gleaming flame. But what dazzled my eyes more than anything else was her cloak, for it was a deep black, glistening with sable sheen;...Here and there along its embroidered border, and also in its surface, were scattered sequins of sparkling stars, and in their midst the full moon of midmonth shone forth like a flame of fire. And all along the border of that gorgeous robe there was an unbroken garland of all kinds of flowers and fruits...Such was the vision, and of such majesty. Then, breathing forth all the blessed fragrance of happy Arabia, she deigned to address me with voice divine.

It is such visions which we seek after in our own dreams. These can be provoked by the regular contemplation of a statue or image; idolatry has been forbidden for this very reason. Regular adoration, performed nightly before sleep is a simple and powerful way to this. You will notice that the goddess when she comes, and she will come, displays other aspects, items, objects and an appearance which must be carefully noted once the vision has passed. These can then be added to your living altar and adorations. Others will work with a living priestess, or mirror.

This is the wreathed vision of beauty, which even Plato in his *Phaedrus* sees illuminating our world from the heavenly (now interpenetrating) other:

But beauty, shone in brilliance among those visions; and since we came to earth we have found it shining most clearly through the clearest of our senses; for sight is the sharpest of the physical senses, though wisdom is not seen by it, for wisdom would arouse terrible love, if such a clear image were granted as would come through sight, and the same is true of the other lovely realities; but beauty alone has this privilege, and therefore it is most clearly seen and loveliest.

As such, we are the disciples of terrible love who have attained such a vision and can through our strength go on to embody it. In working witchcraft it is essential that we reach back through the morphic realm and rediscover and reverence the healing dream. We must survive the burning flames of her theophany and learn to walk in them. It is from dream contact that cult comes. This is the pathway along which oracular vision arises.

The dreams experienced in classical incubation can in addition give instructions on what actions to take to affect the cure. A parallel to this can be found in working with the goetic spirits. The spirit can simply appear and grant our wishes, as in tales of the Arabian djinn, or can give us instructions on further actions and rituals to perform. Just as seeing the emblems or sacred objects in the mysteries reconnects us with our initiation, so the vision of the chimeric demonic can in itself create the change that we seek.

The theophany of light and fire and serpents carried over into the Christian cult. So, we return to John of Patmos, whose whole culture was beset with dreaming. The biblical examples are multitudinous, but every cave also had its nymph. So can Revelation be seen as a series of incubated visions? John's cave is clearly a dreaming chamber, isolated with an additional stone cowl in which he laid his head. In sparce exile he played out through the theatre of his mind's eye the images and predicament of the foundering church and overlaid that with his hatred of woman, and the oracular cults at Ephesus. The women who tied upon their foreheads the legend ΜΥΣΤΗΡΙΟΝ and uttered prophecy were able to access the same state as those in incubation, but were then able to speak as the goddess. They were unchaste of tongue and therefore in Christian terms, whores, aside from any actual sacred harlotry. John sought a vision that encompassed their fall. Powerless, he has only his disciple, the bare rock walls and with his eyesight dimming, the vivid pictures of a story he feels impelled to tell. So, is Revelation a dream vision or dovetailed acacia wood overlaid with gold to appear conterminous and bearing a deceiving angelic countenance?

Revelation is clearly not raw oracular speech. It bears tool marks, they have not been effaced as in poetry to appear effortless, but neither is it simply cipher or naked propaganda. So what is it that John presents to us? As a writer, and highly sensitive to the nuances of text, I find all of these elements present in John. One of the difficulties is the poor Greek of the original (care of Proclus) and the fact that we relate to the sonorous form it most often appears to us in the prosody of the King James Version. There are clearly 'linking passages' so we should perhaps rather than studying the text look at the images, for it is these emblems that encapsulate and I would argue inform the entire vision.

The Jesus of Revelation appears in the same manner as the classical incubation accounts, effused with light, and with a new detail: sword-tongued. There is the tell-tale serpent, three forms of Goddess whom owe much to the great goddess of Apuleius and Inanna. It is these snapshots which arrest our gaze and seek to imprison us within their all too vivid moral colours. John seeks to overwrite and emblazon his meanings upon us, and to do so he has descended into incubation, bringing the culture and stories he knows down with him, but seeing them re-emerge onto the sand-spit of consciousness decked out in gaudulent forms.

However, in this Christian propaganda we are drilled to see ourselves as containing the animating source of both the divine and the demonic, and forced to make the choice. This is the error of dualism. What John cannot grasp is that serpent's venom is the Medicine of God. The serpent courses with the fiery marrow of the deified heroes and the mighty dead. John does not encounter Asclepius as a healing serpent, but shuns him as the enemy, choosing instead the sickness beloved of the world haters. The goddess is rejected. As such no healing is possible, the knowledge of the mysteries is broken apart. John of Patmos has been unable to decipher his own script as anything other than a curse, and so have those who have followed him. I would argue that the curse is deliberate, pervasive and one of our key cultural myths which we need to strip from ourselves if we are to dream true. Ted Hughes shoulders such a task, my understanding of this is given in 'A Spell to Awaken England.' In witchcraft we must embrace the wisdom of the old serpent, the devil, and the goddess with whom he is intimately bound.

This interior art is not one that has come down to us. Perhaps this is also a reason why John has not been seen as a dreamer, the art has been devalued, exteriorised in our culture of surfaces. It seems so simple that it is passed over, an unproductive disruption to a 24 hour economic treadmill, a respite perhaps, but not a doorway. We must understand the war on dreaming not simply from the shelter of the cave, but plot how the shadows of the cross become a forest of aerials and signals that in an even more radical way deny us vision by supplanting our symbols with their own. We cannot simply approach dream as if we are pristine, but must understand the history, violence and distortion that have been done to it. In this way the healing and visionary aspects will return and flood us with renewed meaning. In order to do this I will use the trajectories of the psychoanalysts, surrealists and beats before confronting the morass of mass culture and advertising.

The enthusiasm of Freud and Jung to test the gates is now a parlour game only for the moneyed classes. At one time, it was dynamite. Perhaps the horror of the First World War enabled a breach in the first line of defence, the *thou shalt not* shattered. It gave from the pregnant weight of denial that had been channelled into the Christian Empire, and now liberated by blood, cocaine, female emancipation, wet souls in fox holes, relentless machinery, slaughter. The dream was recognised again and made its demands upon the dreamers for interpretation to be heeded and given value. Healing was sought in dream and its analysis before cheap oil replaced it with what is tellingly referred to by its patients as retail therapy. Even the famous couch replicated the Greek *kline*, the couch used in incubation and gave a name to their practice with the word 'clinic.'

The work of the Viennese magicians was joined by the Surrealists whose planchettes drew words then images on café tables and into art galleries, and wrote out the omnipotence of dreams once more. André Breton's *First Surrealism Manifesto* of 1924 defines the problem they faced:

> In the guise of civilisation, under the pretext of progress, we have succeeded in dismissing from our minds anything that, rightly or wrongly, could be regarded as superstition or myth; and we have proscribed every way of seeking the truth which does not conform to convention.

This critique still stands and we shiver naked and unsated by the images which assail us in their place. Yet as we will see, the response of civilisation to what it characterises as superstition and myth, and we know as witchcraft, has undergone a further transformation. But let us first remember our histories, Breton defines his terms, notably excluding the visual arts, an omission he quickly corrected:

> SURREALISM, noun, masc., Pure psychic automatism by which it is intended to express, either verbally or in writing, the true function of thought. Thought dictated in the absence of all control exerted by reason, and outside all aesthetic or moral preoccupations. ENCYCL. Philos. Surrealism is based on the belief in the superior reality of certain forms of association heretofore neglected, in the omnipotence of the dream, and in the disinterested play of thought. It leads to the permanent destruction of all other psychic mechanisms and to its substitution for them in the solution of the principal problems of life.

Yet even Breton does not insist on the primacy of one method, or as we would say, one vision:

> It is important to note that there is no method fixed a priori for the execution of this enterprise, that until the new order it can be considered the province of poets as well as scholars, and that its

34

success does not depend upon the more or less capricious routes which will be followed.

Austin Osman Spare claims to predate their experiments giving a date of 1901 for his first use of automatism, and corroborated by his published work *Book of Pleasure* in 1913. Yet beneath this is witchcraft, dreambooks, divination, folk magic and the spiritualism of the 1840s. These are the artefacts that get forgotten in the rush to the modern. Perhaps we are embarrassed by the table rappers, mesmerists and tea leaf readers. But these are the impulses that humankind has always responded to. History is a wide wild river with many tributaries often written about as if it were a single channel rifling down an inevitable watercourse to churn the mill of progress.

Dalí's Paranoiac-Critical method was constructed in the 1930s. The aim was to perceive non-linear connections, as paranoids do. The resulting works often contain juxtapositions, optical illusions. He wrote: 'My whole ambition in the pictorial domain is to materialise the images of my concrete irrationality with the most imperialist fury of precision.' His photo-realistic visions have become popular shorthand for the whole Surrealist movement. Yet I sense here a disconnection, perhaps wrought by the trauma of the War, from a whole history of witchcraft that has navigated precisely within this space. The Surrealists are pre-occupied with accessing dream, but not necessarily moving within it – a criticism that applies to the modern entheogen and psychedelic movement who can seem little better than tourists. In fact, we could go so far as to define witchcraft as the art of navigating dream. We are surely trespassing here in the realm of the oracular, and in witchcraft we have the methodology to 'read' this green language with fluency. Not through immersion in the tables of 777 a generation of magicians have confined themselves to, but through a living and shifting relationship to the underlying magical and mytho-poetic reality. If this is paranoia we are indulging in, then it has an illustrious lineage splendidly wrought in heraldry, alchemy and poetry.

The games that the Surrealists played, whether frottage or entopic graphomania, or any of the other delightfully named arrangements, were both a rediscovery of techniques that date from Lascaux, and an admission that the transmission had somehow been terribly damaged by the structures of civilisation that we now stood amongst. I would suggest that the example of play, of games, should be one which we enthusiastically partake in. The neglect of this can be seen in the records that list apparent children's games in Sumeria that were only recently understood to be a critical element of the cult of Inanna. We should not put away our childish things, or sacrifice the ludic spirit of youth, and thus forget the way to the divine. It must be recalled that it was the toys of Dionysos − spinning top, knucklebones, bullroarer, ball, mirror, wool − which were the *symbola* of his Mysteries.

Perhaps, dare I say, unconsciously, Dalí and the terminology of the Surrealist movement allowed the medical pathologisation of altered states and artistic production to be seen as the result of personality disorder. The idea still stubbornly remains that LSD places us in the world of the paranoid schizophrenic. Art, and by extension magic, then becomes something of which we can be cured. We have been labelled sick rather than evil. To be rendered harmless is to be rendered powerless. This has perhaps been made easier by the disconnection from tradition that the Surrealists represent, presenting themselves as if they are an entirely novel phenomena. This is not to suggest that the Surrealists did not produce new work, but it did not make the explicit connection to its ancestry. This was a terrible mistake which has been mercilessly exploited by our enemies whose raison d'etre is divide and conquer.

The pursuit of dream did not end with the Surrealists. Neither did it begin with them, here I drop a few frames, Rimbaud's deliberate derangement of the senses ventriloquised through Morrison's lizard lips, Alfred Jarry, Baudelaire, Lautréamont, Blake. We can trace it through to the Beats of the 1940−50s. In the queer descriptive litany of Ginsburg, and who put it better than in *Howl*, the generation were looking for something with what is now unfashionable anger:

angelheaded hipsters burning for the ancient heavenly connection to the starry dynamo in the machinery of night...

But in *Howl*, the enemy, here characterised as Moloch, as demiurge holds sway. This then was an American dreaming, as the dispossessed, the queer, the poet, the artist sought to find meaning beyond the confines of the white picket fence. The open road of gasoline drew them to their secret interiors. Yet they had found the ticket to dreams, the use of visionary drugs and with them the unlocking of their denied sexual identities. I repeat myself, as this repetition is also in the nature of dream. Let us say that a witchcraft with no drugs is no witchcraft at all. The dream can still be found in the lees of the wine cup into which the serpent has miraculously dissolved.

Critically, the Beats looked to the East, neglected and rejected by an American dream wrought by an industry that did not share their tangle of limbs and beards. Perhaps some sought a mythical India where everyone smokes Lord Shiva's weed. But more accurately, they wondered after the ego dissolution and boundlessness of the successful psychedelic session which was not described in their cultural manuals. If it was mere exoticism, this trope needs challenging. But who are we to limit the scope of any dream? America is an empire adrift, a cut-up of cultures that is an alien everywhere. No one more so than William Burroughs, whose name deserves a place in every serious book of witchcraft. He chose the witchlands of Mexico, that American Bardo, and the interzone of Tangiers, before squirming with the cockroaches into the Beat Hotel and 9 Rue Gît-le-Cœur. You have to travel to do this, you have to be the stranger in the pursuit of the dream. So I ask, can we now find strength in our own traditions, but also acknowledge our place at the crossroads? Or we are just flotsam in Goa, on Freak Street, digging our graves in Majorca with every sunrise? Witchcraft offers us the connection we need to be more than desperately criss-crossing the wasteland and perilously low on gas. In a real sense we have become severed from connections, overwritten, cut-up, lost in a globalised symbol set that provides no meaning beyond a message to consume.

Can we find an example that transcends the psychoanalytical, that blends the creative and the magical? A nexus that can suggest a way out of the impasse of simply more drugs, less linear narrative, or increasingly hedonic narcissism? Is there a way back into the dream labyrinth of the witch house? I suggest that we can make such a journey, and that an example of such a life and work is that of the poet Peter Redgrove who with Penelope Shuttle embraced the menstrual mystery of witchcraft and whose method was that of lucid dreaming.

Redgrove had his shamanic awakening in the total submersion of insulin coma therapy. This was prescribed following a breakdown when conscripted into National Service and the unsafe diagnosis of incipient schizophrenia. The technological response to a body out of order was an inquisition conducted in lab coats by lady doctors. A series of submissions, fifty descents in total that dismantle him but give him the poetic gift. Echoes here of Sylvia Plath, who undergoes the voltage of EST and expresses the experience in the shared poetic figure of Lazarus.

Redgrove went through psychoanalysis under the unorthodox John Layard, an experience which he later glossed as being qualified in the methods himself. Certainly he played the Magus at times, both for his deeply inspired college acolytes, and his contemporaries. The answer was not however found in Jung, but in a poetic quest and often obsessive ritual actions grasping towards the mythic. His is an intensely personal body of work.

Critical to us here is *The Wise Wound*, a book written through a profound six month dreaming. It remains a peculiar text, fusing the scientific writing of his first career with the polemical and poetic work that he had awoken to. His partner and fellow poet Penelope Shuttle was wracked by painful periods, and at Peter's behest began to conquer the dream space. Drawing the dreams, describing them, with Peter acting as analyst and psychopomp the images became ever richer. In unlocking the dreams and charting the flow of the menstruum, Redgrove entered the perilous world of witchcraft and together they began to fathom their sexual depths. *The Wise Wound* is both a physiological map of the womb and its periodicity, the magical flow of blood and the knowledge that is witchcraft. Redgrove observes the need for more sleep during menstruation, and consequently a greater demand made by the dreams at this time. He scents magic, pursues it. He understands that this blood is a powerful magical salve and applies it. Rather than seeing it as a curse, menstruation is celebrated as a time of great creativity and sexual desire. For him, this is the peak moment. It is the very opposite of what culture was saying at the time.

I do not share all the conclusions of Redgrove, whose focus is upon the black goddess who sends dreams, the alluvial enfolding mother. This, in combination with his reading of Grant's exegesis, his understanding of kabbalah (with special emphasis placed at the throat, Daath), and his personal ritual complex 'the game,' leads him to equate the non-procreative sex during menstruation with the sabbat.

His sex magical approach can be studied in *The Black Goddess and the Sixth Sense*, where the adepts Frater S.C. and Soror S.M. whom he purports to interview are in fact Penny and himself. He writes:

> men and women together did indeed produce an elixir, and it could be tasted. Sometimes is was like honey, sometimes metallic. Sometimes it fizzed on the tongue like champagne. It could be made at the various culminations of the menstrual cycle, usuallly signalled by the female partner's sexual 'high'...

He goes on to explain how after the final climax they would merge 'into dream and hypnagogic states, and back again.' This is part of how dream and sex and poetry and witchcraft form a perfect circuit. This is a creative way out of the impasse.

Redgrove is able to combine the mastubatory excess of his mud-daubed sexual awakening, through the plunge pool of the insulin coma and, as an adult, integrate all these into a menstrual mythology, worked out in prose, poetry, plays and texts written at a dizzying lick under auto-hypnotic suggestion, or seen through the glassy wash of booze. What might be personal peculiarities enable him to unsqueamishly seek after the dark moon mysteries, which he does as a lover. This is different to many male writers who act as if menstrual blood is something which they have access to by virtue of their special knowledge. They demonstrate a sense of entitlement that sees the body of the woman as something that they own, an alchemical dispensary and means to their end. Redgrove does not come across as such a man.

Redgrove and I would agree at the lunar eclipse, clearly a bloody moon, but I think that he is mistaken in some of his logic, driven as he is by the menstrual imperative. This goes to the core of the mythic structure which this book will gradually unfold, and my very different conclusion.

It is important to acknowledge the centrality of *The Wise Wound* in the modern history of witchcraft, a book which inspired one of the other important texts in my own mythic reading, Chris Knight's *Blood Relations*. I do not see my own understanding of witchcraft as antagonistic to these other texts, but perhaps it will enable them to be read with new eyes. For the earth, the blood, the corporeality of witchcraft, the ritualistic sexuality, we must pay our debt to Peter Redgrove, as his biographer Neil Roberts incisively titles him, a lucid dreamer.

The menstrual mandalas of Shuttle and Redgrove are an example to emulate. A diary and dream book that we write for ourselves. This is the manual of dark moon magic, of necessary introspection, of incubation. Of how the observation and integration of the cycles can unlock powerful creative forces, that allow us to explore both our personal mythologies and to engage in a process which is not merely inward looking. Simple psychology and self-help are pale wraiths in comparison to the boons and dangers of witchcraft.

We must take the history of dreaming back. As we disconnect

we must also reconnect to allow the dream to pour through. I press stop on the recapitulation tape. You can wake up now, we are here in present time.

If there can be a war on dreaming, I propose a devastating counter strike.

Recognise that something sinister has been sculpting the landscape of dream. We are seeing an unprecedented colonisation and colonialisation of the dream worlds. When we discussed incubation it was made clear that the ancient world understood the importance of dream, and since then it has been accumulating a grey silt. The dream world is becoming as polluted as the natural world, as despoiled. Before we even reach the Asclepium, our minds are chorusing with chatter, assailed by demands. The previous strategy of *thou shalt not have unauthorised dreams* has been superceded by a more terrible strategy. It is not simply dream which is derided as meaningless, but every aspect of our lives. In a parody of Hassan Il Sabbah, nothing is true and thus nothing is permitted. We parade our inner selves which are revealed to be no more than loyalty to a sect of compatible brands. When we see ourselves and the world around us we do not recognise the sacred. Our culture has devoured itself. It is little wonder that Christianity sees the end of days, that Islam retreats to medieval certainties, that everyone else is plugged into their digital soma slavery.

Dream is in competition, not simply with the force flash frames of John, but with a far more sophisticated machine. Though psychology has been mocked, it is the tools of Freud and Jung which are used to mine our desires and insecurities in an incessant and morphing propaganda assault. We must avail ourselves of the work of Edward Bernays, MKUltra, Project Artichoke. These are the modern heirs of the inquisition whose desire to mould us has not ended in the sniper scopes of Manchurian candidates but in drone-war and advertising campaigns run on military lines. They do not wish us to read their plan it is Majic, Top Secret, Eyes Only. We are only meant to watch the spectacle as it wraps around us with the greasy over-intimacy and forced rapport of a salesman. A designed re-arrangement of our senses is underway to make us not citizens under Cæsar, not simply betrayed by our lust, but alienated from nature and sold a narcotic spectacle that sickens us even as we ceaselessly consume. Witchcraft opposes this.

The old TOPY proverb goes: *our aim is wakefulness, our enemy is dreamless sleep*. Yet the dream has been hijacked with a slew of more insidiously compelling visions. We are pitted against an industrial culture which fabricates our dreams for us and insinuates them through our culture and our language. How can we dream when our vocabulary of symbols has only the nuance of newspeak? These are spectres of desire and though marked for sale, remain unattainable. Our culture is as sick as the planet which it is gnawing to the bloody core. We have attained the dreamless sleep state in that our symbols are dictated to us by advertising more effectively than they were even by the Church. But wait, restate, these dreams dreamt for us are destroying the very fabric of the planet. They are the projection of a civilisation in utter crisis. In a terrifying circle we are being forced into deeper dream to cope with this. As witches we must dare to confront this rather than seek comfort, we must pass the test of the gom jabbar. We must look at our world as it is, and it is a desperate and painful ordeal to undergo. Yet the pain of the world is what we are masking by accepting the false dreams of our fallen empire whose jaws still devour even in its death throes. Before dream we must open our eyes, and wash them clean.

The modern world is an exercise, not in incubation, but rather isolation and fragmentation. We offer an alternative, the sabbat at which the dreaming cells convene and are shared.

This process will not go unopposed. The inheritors of John wish to bar the gates to numinous experience. Remove value from vision, disenchant, dispossess, criminalise and marginalise what is at the heart of human experience. This is the poison path, that of cognitive sovereignty, we plainly state that we will gain control of our dreaming. Witchcraft says, we will not cut out our own hearts. The dreaming draughts can be sought. Visions that leach the false colours from our enemy's faces are waiting.

The thaumaturgy of our enemies has evolved, but we have stratagems to apply against them. Witchcraft asks us to dream the un-permitted dreams, of which the sabbat is the highest form. We will reach the high places together as the Simurgh, not as competing cults, but with a mutual recognition that we are all on the path of the wise. Here then, is the stratagem.

First we must disconnect from the artificial vision of the spectacle. A simple step is this, get rid of your television. Next, delete yourself from the digital. Gain control of the data which is being used to keep us in a feedback loop of signal and the narcotic of approval. The much vaunted flow of information is simply noise. It actively colonises our short term memory by overloading its processing ability. We must turn it off if we wish to dream again.

We must engage in self-reflection free from media, or we are mere reflections of another's dreams, a branded patina that shifts to disguise our inner emptiness.

Witchcraft is oversocialised, to use Ted Kaczynski's term, and I make no apologies for going to such radical and misrepresented thinkers. The supposed elders of witchcraft are engaged in the same process as the oversocialised leftist that he rails against in the quote below. First read the text as it is, then substitute the word *black* for *witch* and read it again:

The oversocialized leftist shows his real attachment to the conventional attitudes of our society while pretending to be in rebellion aginst it. Many leftists push for affirmative action, for moving black people into high-prestige jobs, for improved education in black schools and more money for such schools; the way of life of the black 'underclass' they regard as a social disgrace. They want to integrate the black man into the system, make him a business executive, a lawyer, a scientist just like upper-middle-class white people. The leftists will reply that the last thing they want is to

43

make the black man into a copy of the white man; instead, they want to preserve African American culture. But in what does this preservation of African American culture consist? It can hardly consist in anything more than eating black-style food, listening to black-style music, wearing black-style clothing and going to a black-style church or mosque. In other words, it can express itself only in superficial matters. In all ESSENTIAL respects most leftists of the oversocialized type want to make the black man conform to white, middle-class ideals. They want to make him study technical subjects, become an executive or a scientist, spend his life climbing the status ladder to prove that black people are as good as white. They want to make black fathers 'responsible,' they want black gangs to become nonviolent, etc. But these are exactly the values of the industrial-technological system. The system couldn't care less what kind of music a man listens to, what kind of clothes he wears or what religion he believes in as long as he studies in school, holds a respectable job, climbs the status ladder, is a 'responsible' parent, is nonviolent and so forth. In effect, however much he may deny it, the oversocialized leftist wants to integrate the black man into the system and make him adopt its values.

I am not suggesting that witchcraft places us in the invidious position of blacks. Such victim mythology is simply exteriorised self-loathing by the privileged, and if you are a white male in the Western world, that is exactly what you are, privileged; women have it harder. We must reject the values of our culture, and actively oppose them with the visions we garner from dreaming. Many of the elders of the craft have however played a 'responsible game' that is anathema to witchcraft itself. But this is also a critique of those witches who simply think it is a matter of listening to 'witch-style music' wearing 'witch-style clothes' and thereby achieving nothing at all. It does not matter if you listen to black metal or Bach, the proof of witchcraft is the rejection of the values of this culture and the actions that you then take. Where you sleep is where you dream from.

Apocalyptic witchcraft is not limited to any single ideological approach. It is as diverse as dream itself, though united in its difference and distinction to the dominator culture. With every affirmation of the sacred interconnectedness, the participation in the erotic flow of life we move into a real world, the world of nature from which we are profoundly alienated. There is a realisation that the cut up, sold, owned and despoiled world is both interior and exterior.

So let us having lost those frightened by even the idea of disconnection whisper the next stage in the process, the realisation that it is not a disconnection it is in truth a process of enchantment. As dream opens to us again it does so with a new understanding that we are part of the world, not seeking escape from it. We are able to read the symbols of dream in a life lived which is shot through with mythic significance. This vision is derided by our culture, but once we are free from the demands of incessant feedback loops and approval seeking behaviour, the derision has no power over us. We have awoken from the spell of thaumaturgy and the Prospero's begin to quail. Here the regular practice of the dream diary will keep us safe. Here the friends and lovers we have will be shown for what they are. Expect change.

The third step is to deepen. Having stepped outside of the official narrative to regain the sacred, the rose garden game begins in earnest as we chart our personal labyrinths not those woven on the industrial dream looms. Demands for purification arise, of the fast, purging, dietary changes. We begin to know ourselves apart from what we have repeated by rote. Now is when we begin to realise the full potential of incubation. Now we begin to become self-aware in dreaming. Now we are prepared for that different dream. We travel further, to a shared inner landscape that lies beyond the shallow brackish dreams of the day's events. This is the *kur* of the perfumed cedars. Before we depart for the sabbat, we will seek the vision of its Queen. It is at this level of dreaming that she reveals herself to us. There are aids, of which mugwort commends itself, as do tinctures of poppy, solvents of mandrake wine, mushroom, Syrian rue and polygala root.

It would be a grave injustice to the history of witchcraft if we were to see these as artificial in some way. We need this lore which is an adjunct to the work, not an alternative. We must return to first principles and make careful preparation of ourselves as the precious vessels of dreams. We must navigate the inner landscape that spreads from pillows to streets to meadows to hills and rises through forest to the very mountain peaks. She is not simply waiting. She comes for us.

From the intimacy of this exchange begins the process of becoming oracular, of being the heart and tongue. We can call this what it is, possession, and with this the gift of prophecy. When this is attained you will be able to do more than engage in private ritual, you will embody the mythic. Oneiromancy spills over and with utterance and action changes the world.

We are such stuff as dreams are made on. Dreamers, awake.

IV

This dance for Inanna
Cross matched
The lipstick line split
Turning ropes, hawsers and cords,
The triple twisted skein
Heaven, earth and underworld
Is bound
Cat claw tight
To lion bridle, dragon snare
Worn slinked about her hips

A ſpell to awaken England

When the modern mediumistic artist looks into his crystal, he sees the last
nightmare of mental disintegration and spiritual emptiness...
But he may see something else ... the vital, somewhat
terrible spirit of natural life, which is new
every second. Even when it is poisoned
to the point of death, its efforts
to be itself are new in
every second.

Word blind we miss the blood essence of magic. The poets do not
repeat, they reconnect. They do not search out the words, rather
the words come out of them, screaming like crowned mandrakes. It
hurts to do this work. To be cursed to find the spell that will awaken
England.

There are well known works, *The White Goddess*, for all the flaws,
keeps trapping us in letters twisting out of the damp trees – factually
flawed, but more convincing than Spare's knotted stillborn alpha-
bet. The idea insists that there is a secret tradition and that it can be
riddled out of the sphinx-grip of verse. That poetry is a better guide
to history than the flayed documents of the scholars. For all the
disapproving head shaking, Graves gave birth to a tradition, passing
through Cochrane into witchcraft. Cochrane finds the belladonna
which flares open the iris, to let in more beauty, more light, with
which to witness that terrible end to all riddles. It cannot be ex-

pelled, the message kills the messenger. The oracle gives the same answer to each new seeker.

But Graves I sense failing, that deer palpitation, that reedy voice of ancestor receding. The myth no longer vital in this telling, falling away. The old king in the grove waits in vain to be slain and passes into muttering decrepitude. Where are those that dare to seek the thicket? It is not the myth that falls out of date, it is the way of wording it. New voices are endlessly needed to swell their throats with song. Poetry is the unbroken lineage.

Peter Redgrove emerges from the corrosive salt baptism of the lost peninsula, with Shuttle, to braid the bloody flux into menstrual myth and poems. Hard atmospheres shake his skull into brave speech, new utterance. The two revolve weighted and resonant. Here be witchcraft. A thing part art school and part scavenged from the flotsam of the Western tradition, illumined by intimations of Tantra pried from the eldritch fingers of Kenneth Grant. From this, a Jacob's ladder is fashioned and found that leads back up to the witchhouse door. Sex becomes dangerous again when the artists have it, remembering what it means beyond the veil of repression and the mere mechanics of pornography. *The Black Goddess and the Sixth Sense* has unfinished business with us, a shrine still not venerated, or fully understood, *The Wise Wound* resurrects the female sex. A phosphorescence clings to the image of Peter and Penelope, a spectral spindrift. Their work is a considered magical inclusion in *Datura*, launched at the witch museum like a spell in a bottle to rupture its seeds on another shore.

My own — or better spoken, her — book is a deliberate part of this sequence of black, white and red. Again, history, scripture and poetry is rent into revelation. Dramatically slashed, perfumed and intoxicated, the seed pearls and rubies and red gold blush on her living skin. We can retell but not repeat, each storyteller must make the tradition come to life. Where is your proof? is the demand of the goddess. Again, show the trick to me again. Make me laugh. Make me smile. Arouse me with the way you put together your words. Show me that you mean it.

We are the disenchanted generation, and much in need of poetry. Vowels drawled in speech and eclipsed in txt. Even these poets and their quest, so close, are an ossuary of skulls rolled smooth as river stones. Their language becomes incomprehensible as we atrophy into predictable texts and catchphrase cadences. The terrible names of goddess are being erased. What I seek in poetry is the transfiguring shock of vision. It is rare, so rare that we have taken it upon ourselves to both publish and write it.

Yet magic, never caught in the nylon filaments of sigils for long, slips back and fights against the current. It assaults the weirs with a drama and passion that few see, lost in their own reflections mistaking the depth of still pools for the reflections racing on the surface. The poets go on heedlessly, plunging their heads into the flow, gasping back to the source of all things as their blood suffocates in exertion. It is poets who are hunting the myth, the song, the spell to awaken England from dreamless sleep. It only takes one voice to recite it into life. As Ted Hughes says, repeating Eliot, repeating the poets before him, it must be read aloud. I add, and with emotion.

I have my own litany of lost saints to recite. As Graves fades out, as Shuttle and Redgrove begin to be rediscovered, I ask that you hear one more hagiography. This one passed over already, a tale that is neglected perhaps for a celebrated death and the after echo, chambered in the second barrel. Some biography is inevitable as his poetry is shot through with it as surely as thick quartz veins craze granite. I will not gild the sepulchre. There are great chunks of poetry as awkward and looming as the man himself. Sequences that fail under the weight of the images they are bound to. There is the mawkish monarchism from his Laureate obligations that should have been struck off at the neck, a bardic obligation gone awry. Then there is *Crow*, the unresolved cast out in Leonard Baskin's gnarled brass and scrawling inks. The anti-hero splitting skulls and laughing at it all, is fated to be unfinished and ragged edged. For all the alchemy of *Cave Birds*, it is the nigredo which we must always first undergo and then return to. This work, this man, speaks to me, of my own childhood growing adult in the wilds, of the massy weight and dread of writing that cannot be expelled.

A nature poet some say, and those raw vistas of the untamed are too much for many. The savage extravagances of *Crow* the hunched belligerence of *The Hawk in the Rain* the delicacy of spiders to the most sluttish of sheep render a nature that is more primal than is proper. This has led some critics to suggest that Ted Hughes has no supernatural, only nature, but that is to mistake the signature and voice of the goddess who is ever present in his work. Those that have eyes will see her. In *Myth and Education* he writes of the interdependence of the outer and inner worlds:

> We are simply the locus of their collision. Two worlds with mutually contradictory laws, or so they seem to us to be, colliding every second, struggling for peaceful coexistence. And whether we like it or not our life is what we are able to make of that collision and struggle.

Like Blake and Lawrence, he has the vision to hold both worlds in his gaze. His hawks and pike are angels, his black Bull Moses a God. This is deliberate rather than a poetic conceit. In a staggering letter to Derwent May he confides and clarifies on the true identity concealed in the poems, Hawk as Horus, Pike as Archangel Michael, Crow as Bran: *I don't just jot things down you know. If I can't bring them out of the pit I don't get them.* This is the much vaunted esoteric, the green language, spoken with fluency.

Hughes sees beyond the social into an ecology which he has hunted and gutted, but crucially worshipped and given tongue to. As dog to his elder brother's gun, there is horror, not of an urban onlooker but of a country man mired in blood. You cannot say that you have a totem until you have lived as both its prey and predator. Hughes holds the severed red tail of another needlessly slaughtered fox and it makes you weep. His advice to poets is apt to all who would switch skin:

Imagine what you are writing about. See it and live it. Do not think it up laboriously as if you were working out mental arithmetic. Just look at it, touch it, smell it, listen to it, turn yourself into it.

There is no sentimentality here. We need dirt under our nails and smoke stiffening our hair. We need salt drying on our chests, and bramble snagged calves. We need to strip our fingers of rings and throw them into the lake. We must dedicate ourselves to our forty days in the wilderness rather than our five minutes of fame. Magic must become more savage if it is to have any meaning in the world, any power. Myths are not to be draped about poetry, they come from the very substance of the earth, this is the mask we must wear. Be fierce from this understanding taking root.

Hughes recognises that the destruction of the wild will bring about our own destruction. In an interview in 1970 he rails: 'When Christianity kicked the Devil out of Job what they actually kicked out was Nature...and Nature became the Devil.'

It is this devil whom Hughes intuits is the goddess denied; if only modern witchcraft was this perceptive. This theme of linked destiny is present in his poems from the beginning. In *Mount Zion*, the congregants hunt to exterminate a cricket lodged in the wall in a poem Blake would be pressed to better. His religion was already nature, and Christ was only a naked bleeding worm who had given up the ghost. We may seem a world away from austere Methodist Yorkshire, but we are still in the grip of this murderous rage to destroy our ecology, accelerating now as our resources diminish. It is not simply a religious critique that Hughes develops. It is fuelled by another understanding, hard won from the industrial slaughter of the War, and once again suggested by the work of Robert Graves.

The White Goddess is given to him on leaving school at 17 to go to Cambridge, and it replaces *Tarka the Otter* as his talismanic text. Clambering out of the Calder Valley, the last Celtic kingdom of Elmet, he goes after the goddess himself. Later, in 1967, he will write to Graves that: '*The White Goddess* is the chief holy book of my poetic conscience.' But Hughes also confides in a 1995 letter to Nick Gammage that Graves is removed from the demonic properties of poetry: 'I can't ever feel that he experiences them first hand and recreates them in their own occult terms. Some kind of dry distance always comes between him and the sacred event.' This is a criticism that cannot ever be levelled at Hughes.

Hughes understands that he is split blaming, like Graves did, Socrates and Plato for their abstraction which would inevitably lead to machine guns and death camps. Put simply, we are murdering the Great Goddess of nature herself with our stupid intelligence. Of his later alchemical drama *Cave Birds* he writes: 'My starting point was the death of Socrates and his murder of the Mediterranean Goddess.' We are estranged from the supernatural power of nature, enchanted by our rationalism, stupefied by culture. Out of this division comes poetry. He feels the wound in himself and the need to heal. Again the healing aspect of magic is absent in the writings of many supposed magicians, and shows that they have not understood the essence of the tradition and will remain mere fragments. Hughes has the green vision, and his mossy books are written for the Goddess of Complete Being even as the book of nature itself is being torn up. As he states in *Winter Pollen*:

> But while the mice in the field are listening to the Universe, and moving in the body of nature, where every living cell is sacred to every other, and all are independent, the Developer is peering at the field through a visor, and behind him stands the whole army of madmen's ideas, and shareholders, impatient to cash in the world.

We cannot remain in alienation, gazing at the wreckage of the road ahead. We must both heal the wound, and not simply prepare for war, but know we are on the battlefield. This is not a retreat into pastoral idyll and play farms. This is nature to split concrete, crack helmets, strengthen our limbs. The crimes against it are crimes against the goddess, against ourselves, and scream for bloody vengeance.

The radical ecological side of Hughes is also present in his children's books, *The Iron Man* and *The Iron Woman*, again wielding myth to impress upon those who as children can still see the insanity of polluting and destroying our world. We must retell this story and with urgency, teach the next generation the words of the spell. Science is not magic, it is murder, a relentless disenchantment that we must all counteract. Here is one part of the spell, inserted for you like a barb in childhood: Again, again, again.

Hughes ceases studying literature after a visitation by a burned and bloody human-handed fox that delivers the pronouncement, *Stop this, you are killing us.* This theriomorph is a magical messenger, not some prim angel made out of too many books, but a nature spirit. Poetry is not to be dissected to death, and neither is magic nor, for that matter, sex. Perhaps his most famous poem, *The Thought Fox*, which alludes to this encounter, can be taken as the litmus test as to whether you will find a way into to his writing, or if the rhythms jar and the assault on the senses comes too blunt. It is the fox that recurs in his work and life at critical junctures, peering from an overcoat on Chalk Farm Bridge, becoming wolf, watching the poet change. He learns to be sensitive to these intrusions, deciphering the tarot of their meanings. Totem is not selected, it is given.

Dropping English in his final year, the wisdom of the decision is confirmed by his choice of a new subject. Archaeology and anthropology provide him another word to conjure with, *shaman*. He asks:

How can a poet become a medicine man and fly to the source and come back to heal or pronounce oracles?

This is not some new-age affectation. Hughes continues to pursue the literature and accounts of anthropology with a vengeance for his entire lifetime, rather than settling back into pipe-and-moccasins complacency. This is a poetic quest, and it endures to the end. The world of the shaman is not an easy one. Crow is the darkest heart, laughing at human suffering, destroying all illusions. But there is no self-pity, rather a need for regeneration and the acceptance of ordeal which we find breaking free in *Prometheus on his Crag*. In the darkness Prometheus wonders, *Am I an eagle?* Most magicians get no further than this. His shout at dawn to drive away the little birds just serves to waken the vulture. It is only through a long bloody confrontation, of stanza after stanza, facing the vulture that he understands.

> Or was it, after all, the Helper
> Coming again to pick at the crucial knot
> Of all his bonds…?

She is the goddess, but we cannot repeat the answer to the koan, we must survive the experience to honestly pronounce the words. See your name chiselled off your wife's headstone, bury your son, your children, your lovers, be burnt to a cinder. Deal with that magician, be present for that, live through that. Some of you will have been here, had your own torments — she must like you.

Nature is not malevolent, it is other. No one chooses to be shaman, it is thrust upon us. It is the bloody head devouring our endlessly regenerating liver. It is the ring-moat of toothmarks on his cheek that marked him out for love. But poetry is getting back up off the canvas when the fight is already lost, when you are already dead. It is the need to fathom out how the disarticulated parts can fit together again, and what is missing. It is all the goddess. Can you recognise her, when she will not respond to your *Come not in that form?* The shock of horror is *duende*, the wound, the critical act in the magical path. This is something that I have written about and ritualised in ordeal, and commend, insist, that it is undergone. All pacts, all poetry, are written in our own heart's blood.

The Bacchae is now atop his stack of talismanic books and remains there. Intoxication, dismemberment, lust, a Dionysiac poetry in contradistinction to Apollo who, stripped of his quiver, is not a plague burst of arrows but academic, anæmic. Hughes has an uncanny way of getting through to the drama of myth that explodes through in his reworking of Ovid. Dictionary in hand, he reveals the sheer power of the moment of transformation. He does not search for obscure words, he thumps the tempo out. That moment depicted again and again on the cave wall when the human skin is being cast off. This is magic and it is beating out the lines, lives and poetry from us all with maddening insistence.

Hughes understands the energies he releases. Writes of poetry as capturing an animal and keeping it alive, sets one poem watch over another, as Blake does with tyger and lamb, innocence and experience. Talking about his jaguar poems to Egbert Faas he relates:

> The tradition is, that energy of this sort once invoked will destroy an impure nature and serve a pure one. In a perfectly cultured society one imagines that jaguar-like elementals would only be invoked by self-disciplinarians of a very advanced grade. I am not one, and I'm sure few readers are, so maybe in our corrupt condition we have to regard poems about jaguars as ethically dangerous. Poems about jaguars, that is, which do have real summoning force.

His poems are all embedded with this summoning force. With the old rituals disintegrating, the energy release is destructive, much as Babalon is seen in Christianity, much as revolt and revolution appear to the old order. Intriguingly Faas has redacted much of the interview, of brilliant and interesting passages at Hughes request, wondering if it was to prevent sending his critics, as Eliot did, off on a wild goose chase after tarot cards and the Holy Grail. I suggest that rather the magician was covering his tracks, that he feared the magical ramifications of letting his words get away. Ann Skea who has gone more deeply into the esoteric aspects of Hughes's work than any other, writes:

> As I got to know Ted better, I realized that this seeming obfuscation of the serious alchemical nature of his work by offering a number of different explanations for its origins was characteristic

of his response to questions which touched on his deeper occult interests. It was not that he denied them. Nor that these other threads of inspiration and meaning were not also part of his work. It was more that like any serious worker with Alchemy, Cabbala, or any other so-called 'magic,' he needed to judge the seriousness of the question, and the purpose and the state of understanding of the questioner.

Yet the spoor tracks across the page, the musk clings heavy. We can hunt out his hermetic cabbala, the numbers he uses, the sequencing of alchemy, but first before finesse we need the rawness and at the end of the operation it must be revealed again vitally intact. This generation has no choice but to give voice to the summoning force. It is not a wild goose chase, but a dangerous quest. How then can we proceed? Hughes has an answer for us.

The ultimate method to balance the forces he finds is the one he began with: myth. In doing so, Hughes sets his shoulder against the Audens, the Larkins and the whole blank alienated intellectualism of the modern enterprise. As magicians we are doing the same work. Our culture is hostile to the numinous, disenchanting nature that it might be destroyed, splitting man and woman into consumer slaves selling us the grave goods of industry. It is time that we made our spells potent in song and deed, make terror our ally. Hughes relates that: 'The inner world separated from the outer world is a place of demons, the outer world separated from the inner world is a place of meaningless objects and machines.'

I suggest that we befriend and bring back the demons, the abominations, the jaguar spirits and with them destroy the machinery that is murdering us, singing meaning back into things. Yet we must also face up to our own complicity, our own guilt. The confession must be made. We are not somehow set apart from this, as some of the egocentric approaches to the left hand path suggest, we are inseparable. There can be no self-deification unless we undergo change. Entropy is not attainment.

Myth has the power of all human experience. It cannot be discounted. Hughes is not passive in the process; he identifies false myths such as George and the dragon, where nature as dragon and woman is slain, again a Revelation motif. He also seeks the myth of myths, that of the healing quest, which is in direct conflict with technology and Christianity which only destroy. The thesis of *The Red Goddess* is the same. He challenges us to take part, though this vital driving energy in his work is often subsumed by the tragic cult of Plath, where Hughes is cast as demiurge and his true vision of the goddess caricatured as misogyny. Nothing could be further from the truth. It is his uncompromising goddess who is behind all witchcraft, though few dare to face her, settling instead for the Virgin Mary clad in pentagram and coddled in softest harm-none velvet. But harm is essential for without it, there can be no healing. She seethes with serpents of malefica. The truth he grapples with spaded hands is the recognition of goddess in wild nature, something Graves was too frail to embody and modern Paganism still too timid to pronounce. Be frightened, she is terrible to behold. Out of the numbness of fear and the pain of the wound will flower recognition and understanding of the deepest of mystery. She is speaking directly to you at all times.

In the life of Hughes, the process of freeing the imagination to engage in the act of transformation is an explicitly magical one. Giving a reading in Norwich in 1978 he states: 'Magic...is one way of making things happen the way you want them to happen.' Shades here of Crowley, whose work he was conversant with, but whose techniques seem often inimical to poetic process. Hughes seems to have preferred the procedural approach of Franz Bardon but has ranged across the entire hermetic canon. He uses elective astrology to choose his publication dates, has enough begrudging skill at the art he even considers advertising his services. In his letters are natal charts, plans for esoteric orders hidden from Arts Council view, enthusiastic endorsement of *The Wise Wound* as the most important book since Graves. My personal correspondence with a witch who met him is telling: 'he was clearly very sure of his own magickal power and not scared to use it.' Like Redgrove he is an active lusty magician engaged in the art, rather than clinical sequencing or the cut and paste of ill-understood symbol.

With Sylvia Plath he hones his method. Whilst *Poetry in the Making* masquerades as a student textbook it has grown from the relentless exercises he devises to break her out of her overly constructed style and free the poetic voice. These are not conventional exercises, the Ouija board chooses titles for poems, dreams are mined, tarot (a birthday present) endlessly spread, the ars notoria pursued. He tells the London Magazine in 1971: 'I was all for opening negotiations with whatever happened to be out there.' They find spirits who keep coming back, with distinct intelligences, quirky personas, dark pronouncements. By applying limits of time, subject et al, Plath is pushed to improvise, something that many magicians are notoriously bad at, and shamans have as their stock in trade. This authentic voice is disguised by the layers of artifice we build up, and these strata must be meticulously and ritually demolished. We must find our own voice, not hide in obfuscation. This is where Crowley and many others fail, for having destroyed one false structure they replace it with another. Poetry keeps us honest, breaks locked orthodoxy.

The horrible truth that Ted has to come to terms with is that the tempest of magical work with Sylvia releases the Ariel voice that destroys her. Though it was there already, Hughes castigates himself for being unable to save her, not having the shamanic power to manage the crisis. Her death is not inevitable, it comes in a series of stacked mishaps. It all stinks of magic. Alas this fractured glass sliver of Plath is pushed back into his heart by those who canonise her as martyr. We must understand these shrill furies as part of the alchemical operation. Both Prospero and Ferdinand and Caliban and Wodwo, Hughes lives out the myths, undergoes the dread initiations. Any magician working with their lover must face these terrible dangers if there is to be any hope; people die from this. Yet he keeps going, finds solace in the simplicity of fishing, stood between worlds in the river midst, sending the fly whiplash over the membrane. The poems flow again. The salmon of knowledge is charmed with hunting songs.

A list of poems in *Birthday Letters* give further evidence, *Ouija*, *The Earthenware Head*, *Horoscope*, *The Minotaur*. Each poem written a time bomb which released the agony of biography from him, and finally acclaim. He is terminally ill. *Birthday Letters* finds us in a dangerous world, of charm, curse and countermeasure. You would not choose to be here. Many find the narrative of this poem sequence the easiest to read, but it is a truly harrowing book of healing. The final uncollected poem has no respite, no answer. It shows him to be the greatest poet we have had since Shakespeare, a magician who has hidden his work in plain sight, followed his spells back to the river source.

But all this skips the critical myth which rises from beneath the churning morass of poetic lineages, resolves itself into the myth of myths, makes all the poems readable, in a book which itself is doomed to never be read. The revelation comes early and 1971 is the crucial year. Writing his introduction to *Venus and Adonis*, the bombshell bursts. The boar that kills Adonis is Venus, transformed into the opposite of her true nature – the Goddess of Complete Being. This *tragic equation* is the myth that suddenly seems to underpin all of Shakespeare's plays. Hughes writes:

> Shakespeare spent his life trying to prove that Adonis was right, the rational sceptic, the man of puritan good order. It put him through the tragedies before he decided the quarrel could not be kept up honestly. Since then the difficult task of any poet in English has been to locate the force that Shakespeare called Venus in his first poems and Sycorax in his last.

With this understanding we can plunge headlong into the chase, the markers have been put in place by Hughes through his reading of Graves. It is Venus, Sycorax, La Belle dame Sans Merci, Nightmare Life in Death, a lineage of English poetry that transmits the sacred myth of the goddess, all rooted in the works of that great bard presiding over England's dreaming: William Shakespeare.

In 1989, by accident, Hughes begins the three year task of writing *Shakespeare and the Goddess of Complete Being*, which literally wrote itself whilst he panted along behind, trying to make it readable. Just as Shuttle, Redgrove and Graves wrote their Goddess texts, Hughes is compelled to add his to the list. His own story is also encompassed in the equation, at one point he considers not publishing *Birthday Letters*, as it has the same magical DNA that is encoded in the *Goddess of Complete Being* but we are all the richer for having both of them.

By identifying *Venus and Adonis* and *The Rape of Lucrece* as containing the entire mythic formula of Shakespeare, he brings a poet's understanding to the corpus, raising it into an organic living body of work. Hughes now is at the height of his powers with the mature experience of his own œuvre to draw upon, his intimate knowledge of encoding the hermetic truths in poetry and prose. He looks at Shakespeare eye to eye in what is a sublime necromantic achievement, the mouths moving in synchrony.

Here is the vision of the boar goddess of the underworld, cribbed from a footnote:

> Her combination of gross whiskery nakedness and riotous carnality is seized by the mythic imagination, evidently as a sort of uterus on the loose – upholstered with breasts, not so much many-breasted as a mobile tub entirely made of female sexual parts, a woman-sized multiple udder on trotters. Most alarming of all is that elephantine, lolling mouth under her great ear-flaps, like a Breughelesque nightmare vagina, baggy with over-production, famous for gobbling her piglets, magnified and shameless, exuberantly omnivorous and insatiable, swamping the senses.

This is not the Venus we have come to expect. It requires us to grapple with uncomfortable ideas and only the structure of myth can aid us, only a lifetime spent obsessed with transformations, with nature, with tragedy, with love can lead us to this point. We cannot do this vicariously. It is our soft groin that is torn and gored by the sickle tusks. Our vaunted magical defences are useless, ploughed through, it hurls us aside, mangled. Hughes' scholar Keith Sagar says of the equation:

> it is far from being some mechanical formula he has invented; it is no less than a complex all-embracing myth, which Shakespeare forged out of his inheritance of classical mythology and gnostic and alchemical wisdom, all transformed in the crucible of his life and times as his supreme attempt to convert apparently random and painful experience into a process of self-transformation.

The equation can be stated relatively simply, but this adumbration cannot reveal the full shadow play that the dense text conceals. Confronting the goddess, the ego can either reject her and seek solace in rationality and self-obsession, or it can embrace her divine love. And here is the rub: it always rejects her. This is the result of the split psyche that the nature poems identify and seek to heal, the division we must confront but do all that we can to elide. Examples of this sequence of events are also played out in the protagonist dramas of *Prometheus on his Crag*, *Crow*, *Gaudete*, et al. This tragedy is followed by madness and the crime against her; *Hamlet* provides the clearest example of this to the lay reader. We can only then be saved by the destruction of our ego and rebirth through surrender to the goddess – in the case of Adonis, as a flower. Three outcomes are possible: an erotic fracture in the hero's carapace caused by her sexual intercession, sainthood, or self-anæsthesia in a living death. There is no arguing about it.

Hughes takes on the mighty task of reading the whole memory theatre of Shakespeare, whom he understands and argues persuasively for as an occult Neoplatonist, into the tragic equation. For this we need to have a magical understanding of the conflict of Elizabethan England, and the mythic dimensions of the civil war. Hughes of course is Laureate under another Elizabeth, seeing the mythic patterns and repetitions. The reign of Elizabeth is an alchem-

62

ical seal where the forces of both Puritanism and Catholicism have their murderous ambitions kept in check, *spell-bound* is the phrase Hughes picks. This became the inner life of the age, as he puts it: 'The ghostly front line of the deadlocked spirit armies of these two giant historical forces was drawn through the solar-plexus of each of Elizabeth's subjects.' Hughes describes Shakespeare's art as a salamander living in this inferno. The forces of civil war are those of Catholicism guised in the sonnet *Venus and Adonis* and Puritanism in *Lucrece*, the point and counterpoint to it. *Lucrece* is in mythic terms the story of Jehovah trying to destroy Asherah, the great serpentine goddess of orgiastic love. These two themes comprise the totality of the equation and fight as dragons under the navel of England, in the crucible Elizabeth has prepared for them. Writing to his copy editor Gillian Bate he acknowledges:

> One can't just refer to this (Occult Neoplatonism) and assume that even Shakespearean scholars will understand and supply the rest. 400 years of cultural suppressive dismissal aren't going to be lifted willingly simply to indulge me.

Shakespeare and the Goddess of Complete Being asks a lot from a modern reader, in what is a truly esoteric text that has also denied the critics safe passage. They do not have the tools to break into it, having failed in the fateful decision where Hughes triumphed by choosing nature and poetry over cold analysis. As readers we can be staggered by the enterprise, feed each new play and poem into the matrix, continue to be fascinated by the insights that we can grasp. I keep going back to it, perhaps like Hughes I can appeal to Sheldrake's morphic resonance, and in publishing this book unlock more secrets. As he advises, we are best to see it as a song, one great epic of bardic text, the endless river of poetry.

As magicians, it is not simply Shakespeare that we can read into this equation, or Rosicrucianism or John Dee, but our own initiation crises. How many have acknowledged their crime, how many let go, how many aim for sainthood? Perhaps when we read the trajectory in the macrocosm we can see why the vision is one of a vengeful fated return, why she demands blood, and every drop at that. The crisis in nature will be visited on man, more rapidly engulfing us than most would think. The equation presages our flowering into apocalypse.

The book is, of course, slaughtered by the vain Adonises whose lines Hughes has delineated so sharply with the tusks of the goddess. He is unswayed, expecting the rejection:

> Any discussion of the book is not about Shakespeare or me – it's about importance of spiritual tradition versus unimportance of it, importance of imaginative life or censorship of same, sterility of artistic life versus abundance of artistic life, the survival of group culture versus the suicide of group culture, depth and reality of psychological life versus academic orthodoxy etc. etc.

This too is part of the equation, this piece some small part of the healing. The day I finished writing this, Hughes took his place in the disorder of Poets' Corner in Westminster Abbey. Again the critics were unable to make sense of his work in their toothless sound bites. But the recognition and stature of Hughes will only continue to grow and with this his magical legacy must not be passed over. Poetry is not an easy birth. Ted Hughes is torn by it, staggering with dark blood running into the dark soil. He is compelled by the goddess. His clotted vision, his hawked up clods of viscera, are the rewards she bestows. A bloody trail for the hunter, writing out his story in a scent trail that the foxes can follow, a heart smashing out irregular rhythm against the ribs, words flung around like crows in a storm, cruel repetitions of fate. Men become wise only by being wounded this deeply. The skulls speak from the riverbed. A resonant choral that turns uncertain beneath our feet. We begin to recite, and with no little urgency, our own composed love songs, a spell to awaken England.

v

The knives are out
Boys locked in halter stocks
Frigged then fenestrated
A choir
For the handmaids of Inanna
Mistress star high-heavened
Looks down
Into the mirror of blood
Smiles at her reflection

The scaffold of lightning

In defining the devil I have had recourse to say this: *the devil reveals a narrow path into a dark wood*. Remember that. He is out in all weathers and seasons in his tatty blacks, but the form is not important. Neither is what kind of crown he sports – horn, thorns, flowers, hat or cap. Nor does it matter that at times he seems the Lord of the World, at others a more intimate, local spirit. It is what he shows us that counts. This definition could be challenged in that the wood has been coppiced and then hacked back to a stand of a few spindled trees. But I will let the phrase stay, as he is this revealer, and the wood is waiting behind all our eyelids. Blink and you might miss him. Walk abroad and you might meet him. His presence is immanent, the path opens before you.

The traditional formula is simple: kneeling with hair loose, praying aloud for his help. You do not need a book to tell you the words, they are within you. If you wish to place an intercessor between you and your desire, then a tradition already exists for you, it is called Christianity. Witchcraft removes the things which obscure our sight of the narrow path, and this agency, this game, is called the devil.

It is time that witchcraft paid the devil his due. The apologists would have us believe that our only history has been that of misunderstood traditional healers and midwives, burned mercilessly by a fanatical and bigoted church and state. The time for such apologies is over. The denial of the devil is a convenient fiction for those who would trade their power for a seat at the table with the very people whom witchcraft has always been recourse against. Witchcraft was, is, and ever more shall be the heresy of heresies. It is without doubt that some of those tortured repeated what the inquisitors sought, but that does not preclude an appeal to the devil by those who have been failed and abused under the shadow of the cross.

We have become bolder now. Our marginal notes have swarmed into the body of the text, our books bear witness of what was once written only with initials. God is dead, but the Devil lives. It is the lure or the devil that has swollen with priapic vigour to fill the failure of a religious witchcraft predicated on poor, albeit romantic, scholarship and the collapse in the power of the Church in the West. Such a jutting phallus, gleaming and anointed, deserves to be worshipped in all its proud glory. The ritual phallus should be present on any working witchcraft altar. Perhaps we can agree with one point of the inquisitors, that to become a witch requires that we embrace the devil in the most intimate sense. Initiation is sexual, is sex.

For some this will be the memento mori at which they turn back. They find the head of the phallus, however lovingly carved in fig wood or stone, cast in glass, to be the ugliest god. Such is their right to choose. Let us speak plainly. The devil has been lover, but also rapist and abuser, contains the fool, the seducer and the dominator. These are faces we must confront, and in unlocking their powers we are taken to dark places that should not be romanticised but can also conceal deep healing. Trauma is here, panic and fear.

It has become widely understood that our relationship with spirit requires pact and not bondage; however, that is not the historical experience. The historical fiction of Michelet makes the lot of the peasant class who are driven to diabolism explicit. In their relentless suffering it made sense to turn to the devil in whom the Church invested ever increasing power. The devil is often tricked by simple ruses, but those who have called upon him are for the most part guided by despair, and the bargains they strike are the kind of indentured servitude that was the lot of the peasant class. They are appeals to a different master, and thus he has often appeared as a demonic aristocrat who whips and beats the witches for infractions, and whose carnal relations with them are commonly given as painful, icy, and non-negotiable. The power relations are not suddenly made equitable but reflect the existing social dynamic. Thus the devil has already doubled, cavorting before our eyes, being both bucolic Pan and privileged Lord.

What we must remember is that the accounts we have, almost always trial testimony, are performed as a penitential theatre of accused, judiciary, nobility and clergy. Such a court is convened on a field of folklore, myth, legend, invention and dream drawn out through torture, threat and false hopes. Rather than discounting all the trial testimony, the latest generation of scholars are daring to suggest that the devil is not simply the misogynist fantasy of the tor-turers, but that he had an existence amongst the folk which the elite demonologies had to take account of. The devil is thus a dialogue, rather than a closed book. This is borne out by the work of Éva Pócs on Eastern Europe, and Emma Wilby on Isobel Gowdie. In her eloquent work, Wilby reverses what had been the previous wisdom of the academy. She writes:

> Increasing interest in the folkloric dimension of witchcraft beliefs is leading scholars to consider that confession-depiction of the Devil might be rooted in genuinely popular ideas about embodied folk spirits, such as fairies and the dead.

Note the use of the word *embodied*. It gives the devil an existence that is recorded, experienced and blooded in the folk and land. We do not need to imagine him out of alien imposed myths of fallen angels. This does remain a mixed heritage, as Pócs observes:

> Church demonology – while taking on board many folkloristic features and absorbing a whole host of the demons of folk belief

systems — itself had an impact on folk belief. These popular devil figures stand somewhere in the middle of the crossfire of reciprocal influences.

The devil must then be considered an aggregate, or to use the classic phrase, legion. He is rustic, and nobility, a confidante and a deceiver, a liberator and a cruel master. We cannot parse these to form an identity which we feel comfortable with. To do so would be as misguided as to sever the paired contradictions of the Thunder Perfect Mind. Each of us must come to our own private resolution of the matter at hand.

If we can argue for the phenomena of a modern witchcraft, it would be disingenuous to deny the fertile growth of new strains of diabolism and witchcraft which owe more to the passion of Michelet and Parsons and the compromising evidence of European demonology than to idealised pastoral forms. Others have simply drawn on their own remnant folklore in its most redacted form, that of mass culture. Rather than rejecting those who reject the false gods and ally themselves with the opposer, we should be listening to the impulses that drive them. A revolutionary youth will always grasp the shape of the future and gallop towards it on shaggy thighs, whether their elders approve or no. The mistake made is often inversion, a potent formula of witchcraft in itself, but one that after breaking the social bonds often simply reforges them and chains its adherents to a dualistic script. This is fatal. The empty pursuit of appetite makes those who show such promise no more than consumers, easily manipulated by their deified desires. The devil has his dangers for all of us. This is the most subtle one as the very keys that deliver our personal liberation can become a guarantee of unbreakable bonds of slavery.

The devil is protean, he changes as we change, our closest companion from the cave to the starry heavens. This is why we cannot leapfrog him to engage with a horned god of our supposed Celtic forebears. Witchcraft is meaningless if we use it to retreat to an imagined past and play at being the very different people who inhabited it. The injunction of the mysteries to know thyself precludes this kind of escapism. The gods of the past came from the soil, the social conditions, and ours must too, none more so than the devil. He paws his way out of the farrowed fields unsettling even the crows.

The devil tells the story of the god of witchcraft in the way that Revelation tells the story of the goddess. It is a slant apertured eye. If the devil is to be any more than a dirty little secret, the thrill behind the acceptable face of the witch god, then we must know the shape of his history. The error most make is recourse to scripture, an unreliable guide at the best of times, and in the case of the devil, truly bewildering. There is no such figure in Judaism. It is not in the Jewish tradition of the wild hairy spirits, but through a very European sequence of slur, fit-up, fascination and fabrication that the enemy is profiled and claims life as his own, as one of us, as amongst us. The devil is a particularly European trickster myth. As this is a polemic, and not an exhaustive history, the reader is advised to turn to the copious primary sources. My work will delineate the features into recognisable shape for the present purpose, and no more. It is by design a succession of rough cuts, cross-hatched that they may yield deeper shadows.

The period of European Christian conversion occurred in a largely rural setting from 300 to 1100 CE, and this is when the horned gods of Northern Europe were demonised. Magic and witchcraft were condemned on account of their Pagan character and in attacks on particular individuals. This period and that which preceded it is viewed with nostalgia by those who would like to inhabit a *what-if* Europe and prize the displaced horned gods as authentic spirits of the land unencumbered by Christian morality. Yet it happened, the effigy of the pale Galilean conquered, not through spiritual force but through political expediency, power, greed and the vinegary truth that must not be forgotten, popular acceptance. Though we are drawn back to find the first forms, we must begin in the now rather than the might have once been. The old gods still speak, but they must do so with young voices. Every age needs the devil reborn, not complacency or nostalgia, but paradoxically the experience of this truth can transport us vertiginously back to a confrontation with the origins of who we once were and who we can truly become.

The Cathars, who walked in step to their eye-gouged holocaust in the Albigensian Crusade of the 1200s, are often considered formative in the creation of the later witch cult. The propaganda against them had raged in advance. In 1179 Allan of Lille baptised the Cathars with the false etymology of *cat,* from the Latin *cattus,* which seems to have been a popular slur, and added that they kissed the posterior parts of a cat, who was Lucifer in disguise. Walter Map, in 1182, seems to have relished giving this spurious account of their activities:

> About the first watch of the night, when gates, doors and windows have been closed, the groups sit waiting in silence in their respective synagogues, and a black cat of marvellous size climbs down a rope which hangs in their midst. On seeing it, they put out the lights. They do not sing hymns or repeat them distinctly, but hum them through clenched teeth and pantingly feel their way toward the place where they saw their lord. When they have found him they kiss him, each the more humbly as he is the more inflamed with frenzy – some the feet, more under the tail, most the private parts. And, as if drawing license for lasciviousness from the place of foulness, each seizes the man or woman next to them, and they commingle as long as each is able to prolong the wantonness.

This worship of the devil as an animal, the sensual sexually assertive foreign feline, was to wind its tail around the legs of the witches. Many found that they liked it. The ideas of a synagogue, *orgia* and *osculum infanum* were also to persist. The state always finds it expedient to criminalise private gatherings, and ascribe the worst deeds to those who partake in them. But this does not prove that such nocturnal events never took place, even if the Cathars themselves were perfectly blameless.

In 1321 attacks began on lepers and Jews, who were accused of poisoning the wells and spreading disease in a universal plot against Christendom. The method ascribed to them was the use of a spectrally potentised chemical weapon, a powder compounded of human blood, urine, three unspecified herbs and a consecrated host. It references the widespread folk magic use of the host both smuggled from the Communion and employed with the complicity of clerics that the central authority of Mother Church now wished to curtail. This is the kernel of truth about which the lie was formed.

The link between the lepers and Jews was a repetition of the claims Josephus had refuted in his 1 CE text *Against Apion*. The Jews were alleged to have their origin as lepers who were expelled from Egypt in an inverted version of Exodus, and in addition worshipped a wild ass or donkey which had led them from the wilderness. Again, this is the devil in animal form. Some of the conspiracy theories had the Jews and lepers directed by the Muslim king of Granada or the sultan of Babylon. These outrageous claims were sealed with the persistent blood libel, that is, the performance of human sacrifice. Josephus relates the version told by Apion of the Temple in Jerusalem: 'they used to catch a Greek foreigner, and fat him thus up every year, and then lead him to a certain wood, and kill him, and sacrifice with their accustomed solemnities, and taste of his entrails, and take an oath upon this sacrificing a Greek, that they would ever be at enmity with the Greeks; and that then they threw the remaining parts of the miserable wretch into a certain pit.' Josephus goes on to debunk the story, yet this monstrous tale persists and gains other features. The Greek sacrifice becomes a Christian child and the blood is kneaded into the Passover bread. The Jews met secretly to do this at a Synagogue or Sabbath. These elements were transposed onto the supposed witch cult. It is important that we know the origin of these tales, as they are repeated as evidence in all such panics down to our day. The arrival of plague in Europe in 1347 saw the Jews blamed again and the litany repeated to devastating effect.

But wait, is this too convenient an explanation which masks another deeper truth? What if the slurs levelled at the Jews, Cathars et al were also folkloric ideas that describe in some sense the action of witchcraft? We should all know by heart the *Canon Episcopi*, and the text behind it, the 906 *Instructions for Bishops*, which reads:

> One mustn't be silent about certain wicked women who become followers of Satan, seduced by the fantastic illusion of the demons, and insist that they ride at night on certain beasts together with Diana, goddess of the pagans, and a great multitude of women; that they cover great distance in the silence of the deepest night; that they obey the orders of the goddesss as though she were their mistress; that on particular nights they are called to wait upon her.

Here with swiftly beating hearts we are exposed to the reality of the witch cult. A pan-European phenomena of night flight, animal trans-formation, and as the accounts progress, the devouring of beasts and men who are then brought back to miraculous life when their bones are wrapped in the flensed hides. If our witchcraft is not simply a repetition of libel, but a folk survival: so too is the devil. If he were not so, the tale would not have captured the imagination of church, state and public enough to stomach the excesses that were carried out against him. Ginzburg, in his *Ecstasies,* confirms this:

> In the image of the Sabbath we distinguished two cultural current, of diverse origin: on the one hand, as elaborated by inquisitors and lay judges, the theme of a conspiracy plotted by a sect or hostile social group; on the other, elements of shamanistic origin which were by now rooted in folk culture, such as the magic flight and animal metamorphosis. But this juxtaposition is too schematic. The moment has come to acknowledge that the fusion between the two lodes could only have been so firm and enduring in so far as there existed a substantial subterranean affinity between them.

The mistake is to think that cult survived in more than instinctual forms as ritual proscription. It manifestly did not, and those who

73

seek to create such structures and clothe them in antique garb are acting dishonestly. The essence of witchcraft is to be found in shamanism, in ecstasies which are choreographed by the devil whom we have called Pan, Hades, Odin and king of the fairies. Our tradition is one in constant creative flux.

In this early period the sabbat is a phantasmal dream experience, it is oneiric, and has not congealed into the physical gathering which was needed to lead to the condemnation of the lepers and Jews as it had with the Cathars. It is from these despised sects we encounter elements of our witchcraft: the sabbat, the persistent blood libel, the orgiastic sacrament, the denial of Christ, the animal god. These elements may well have already existed, but it is with these pogroms that they gained new significance. Evidence was fabricated by the state against any group it chose to attack, a crusade and a methodology that continues to this day.

The Renaissance saw a change of emphasis, as Europe became more urban, with magic and witchcraft now cast as demonic and heretical. Though the pagan iconography persisted to give form, the character of the attacks was changing. Witchcraft was not the imagined or objectionable practices of individuals, but a very real conspiracy headed by a devil whose cohorts thronged the air. Any discrepancies in testimony from this narrative are swiftly glossed, even in the trial records. The air clots around the nocturnal meetings of peasants both in revel and revolt.

The turmoil of the late 14th and early 15th centuries turned the milk very sour indeed. Facing social unrest, an enemy was needed to unite the faithful. Thus magic and witchcraft became a demonic cult, an international conspiracy lead by a bearded devil that was both heretical and criminal, with a distinctly Arabic cast. It is from this history that Idris Shah was able to spin his yarn of a direct Arabic influence on witchcraft. This discredited claim is still credulously repeated in some witchcraft traditions today, Shah having gained the ear of both Gardner and Graves. The impact of Arabic magic on the West has still not been explored much beyond *Picatrix* and the lunar mansions (with the notable exception of Charles Burnett), and though influential and inoculated with earlier cult elements is demonstrably not the origin of the craft or its working tools.

The demonic conspiracy theory lead to the rout of the Templars on the following five-points of accusation: threefold denial of Christ and the Cross; kissing of the initiator three times on mouth, and, euphemistically, the navel and lower back; acceptance of 'unnatural' lust; consecration of the measure by an idol or head; and fifthly, not consecrating the host in the performance of the Mass. Each of these has clear witchcraft parallels and valid ritual applications. The further charge that followed was that they were in league with one Baphomet, whose nature and form was as varied as the imagined European ideas of the time as to who or what it was the Moham-medans worshipped. One thing was certain, they were idolators. The reliquary heads, the prison graffiti, the torture testimony get us no closer to the truth, if there is such a thing. We are denied even a reliable spelling that can be submitted in any enlightening way to a cipher. The devil is, in a cultic sense, this disputed idol, the ritual locus about which the fantasy form of the sabbat has been drawn. As if plucked by a whirlwind, the woodcut images dance about this central figure who still defies a final definition, yet whom we know all too well. It is at these crossroads, translocated from lost Jerusalem and before that Babylon, that the witch cult swarms. So many voices and bodies are here, with no division between high and low magic, heretic and mystic, magus and necromancer, warrior monk, magician and witch. Our identities merge and are lost in the dance that we can now properly call the witch cult. Who could preside over such a gathering other than a motley devil?

What is abundantly clear is that witch hunts did not begin with witches, and are thus not avoided by making ourselves harmless or integrating and ingratiating ourselves with the corrupt systems of governance. The Templars, though haughty and high-handed, were hardly an outsider organisation. The accusations are always the same, what counts is how we respond to them, what truths they conceal and can be made to reveal to us. Simply acting out the parody role which our enemies have scripted for us is not a solution. We need greater finesse. Yet when our enemy describes their fear to us with such eloquence, they reveal their weaknesses which we would be foolish not to exploit. It is a game of masks, and ours is heavy with horns that ground us down through our thighs, as we rise from the heart of the earth onto the balls of our feet.

We know who followed the Templars to strappado and stake, I do not need to stoke those coals for effect or delight in laying out the instruments before you. This has been the history of witchcraft, and it is one of false accusation, torture and murder that has brought us to the foot of the gnarled phallus with questions of our own. It has become fashionable to disregard this history as one that just makes us victims. I say that we have plenty to be angry about not simply from the office of the Inquisition but its current repercussions. I say that when we sever ourselves from this root we sever ourselves from the origin of power in the passions. We are part of this story, not because we need to fixate on the pain to feel justified, but because our history embodies lessons which cannot be torn away with iron pincers or blown away as ash on the wind. We endure.

Ignoring the conflicting descriptions of the Templar trial testimony Eliphas Lévi dressed Baphomet up in allegorical alchemical fashion as a winged Sabbatic Goat in his 1855 *Dogme et Rituel de la Haute Magie*. It has been through Lévi, and the subsequent Masonic hoax of Leo Taxil, that Baphomet become the iconic image of the devil even down to our own century. It is this figure in the tarot packs of Rider-Waite-Smith and Crowley-Harris as trump XV. For Lévi this was a mercurial image, an alchemical emblem, the Azoth. His intention was not to deify the transgendered or the queer, and attempts to suggest this fail to understand that almost every deity in the history of the West has been depicted as dual-sexed, including a bearded Aphrodite. We should not make the mistake of a purely literal reading, as it makes us little better than fundamentalists. The beard has been interpreted as meaning the star or luminary (that is

Venus, or the Sun) at maximum luminousity, in the same way that comets are *hairy stars*. This is green language. It would be better to draw a parallel with the punning female figures unearthed by Maria Gimbutas, that from one angle are goddess, with copious buttocks and breasts, and from another, the phallus itself. Or earlier still, the bone wand of Le Placard, whose vulvic base erupts up into phallic blade. Or the sub-incisions of the Aboriginal Australians and the priesthood of ancient Egypt. These get us far closer to the secret that the devil ultimately guards.

To reveal the secret we must next dissolve the baroque accretions of decadent literature, jaded aristocratic orgiasts, and fin de siècle poseurs or we will simply coagulate more disparate elements onto Lévi's already burdened allegorical goat. It should be able to stand shod on its own cloven hooves. Perhaps we should contemplate simply the goat with the candle between its horns, which is phosphorus/Venus, as the proper glyph for witchcraft in rites when the phallus alone will not suffice. This was the solution of the Basque at their Akelarre. Others use the stang here which is commanding in its simplicity but perhaps not the grand guignol which initiation can require and was acted out in the societies of Horsemen and Miller's word. The devil must be present and potent.

As Urban Grandier witnessed, the devil is always found within the convent walls, however elaborate the locks on the doors. Some say that they entice him. By the same mechanism of thwarted desire he invades our disillusioned technological utopia. There is no counter-measure to banish him. The same is true of witchcraft, which periodically tries to sweep him aside. However well-intentioned this may be, it does a grave disservice to the might of our practice. His force prevails in the world because it is constantly renewed. Regardless of how 'white' we claim to be, the devil will always be seen amongst us, the extra place set at the sabbat supper, the other dancer who moves amongst us, the wandering stranger who is already in exile and thus cannot be expelled.

He is the very figure of every age, and this devil gains more light with every passing day. We are not simply impatient, we are running out of time, out of resources, out of hope, and it is only the devil who makes good on his promises. Our plight is becoming desperate enough for this again. He may be as old and deep as time, but when we join with the devil he is pressingly of our era as well. He has answers to our questions that are met with a level gaze. Witchcraft must provide space for such questions to be articulated.

So where does witchcraft now stand in relation to the devil? It is here that we can invoke the idea of exile, an image of our fractured age, and a title of the devil himself. Our witchcraft is clearly not that of our initiators however well-meaning or dubious their own stories of origin. We are for the most part urban, inhabiting unsustainable cities, perhaps never having so much as seen a goat, or even the stars clearly. Our hedges are the buddleia and fireweed choked wrecks of buildings. There is little call for cunning craft when the eye is not given but trained to our mobile phones. We are exiles from the world of nature, and even the Devil can seem distant as Lord of it all as we flit through our fragile grids. Though it would do well for us to pause and remember the teaching of Bernard of Clairvaux:

> The woods and stones will teach you what you cannot learn from other masters.

There is no retreat for us into the pristine wilderness, which is becoming as softly absent from us as a sparrow's heartbeat.

Yet we also have much in common with the period of the witch hunts, namely financial and social collapse born from environmental catastrophes of our own making. This provokes a need for an enemy, an invisible international pervasive conspiracy for us to unite against, vilify, torture and ultimately murder. The Empire's official inquisitors name their devil al-Qa'ida (a suitably corrupted invention of their own intelligence agencies, just as the devil was) with a now symbolically disincarnate head. This Baphomet, peace be upon him, has replaced the McCarthyism reds under the beds scare that the witchcraft of Jack Parsons was born under. The torture by the state continues, and yes, the executions and kill lists of enemies and innocents alike. It would not be inaccurate to call this a Catholic inquisition, it is part of the same extended franchise. We have simply replaced the Church with the corporate state and I predict that a new witchcraft will rise to confront it, with many heads.

The Empire has several other witch hunts which run concurrently. First is the War against Drugs. As witches, our use of entheogens, plant medicine and even organic and home-grown food places us on that watch list. This has become part of the larger War on Terror, the definition of which is steadily expanding as resources crash and those who oppose the destruction of the planet and their own lives begin to take to the streets in greater numbers. The strategic studies departments have already begun to profile us as *druids*, a deep green popular resistance movement of earth based spirituality that decides to fight back. In seeking to simply reconnect with the natural cycles and defend our trees, plants, animals, birds, mountains, rivers and oceans we have become the enemy again. The fall of the Empire which began abroad is returning to the homeland and will again be characterised as a *foreign* or *unpatriotic* heresy.

So who are we, a question the devil unfailingly asks, and why are we here? This is for each of us to answer, but whatever our practice, or intent, we will be demonised. Thus we petition the devil for his aid. We become mask and are called to seek knowledge through ecstasies.

Who then, is this devil? A simple answer will not suffice, the answer is complex, personal, and is the resolution of polarity, a charged word when I use it here. Let us pick up those carved antler bone figurines of Gimbutas, let us contemplate the graven phallus which began this piece, turn it over in our hands, feel its weight. The poet Peter Redgrove had great insight into this mystery. He realised in his own contemplation that the phallus was the image of the goddess herself. It is formed as the inverse shape of her sex. This prescient realisation suddenly reverses everything we thought we knew. The devil is not the hidden hand of history, but has been formed by the glove it wears. The devil then is the operation of wild nature, seemingly as distant from us as any morning star, but as closely bound to us as our own shadow. The devil is a sign that She is here, as the path into the hidden wood the devil indicates and down which the witch must walk.

VI

Venus phosphorus flare
Mounts and blooms
The battlefield lit
Animals and men
Look up then flee
Bunker busting rays
All will be made clean
When she comes
Pour it out for Inanna
The sun has gone
To death in the west
A new queen risen rules

The children that are hidden away

Then I went to the heath and the wild,
To the thistles and thorns of the waste;
And they told me how they were beguiled,
Driven out, and compelled to the chaste.

The sabbat is the love feast of the witchcraft. It is the central rite by which we have been both identified and condemned. Our revels have been daubed in the blackest garb, the most terrible acts that humanity can visit upon itself, namely incest, infanticide, cannibalism and murder. These exert a fascination upon the popular imagination, which still seeks a salacious glimpse of the proceedings that coalesce in this one spectacular field of nocturnal action. This list of atrocities is why many modern proponents of witchcraft have been quick to distance themselves from what has been considered a demonological imposition upon a simple folk faith.

The thesis, proposed by Carlo Ginzburg, that there is an archaic survival of the pre-Indo-European and the shamanic in the night flight and battles of the *Benandanti* has been welcomed, almost as an alternative to the grand guignol of the Inquisitorial scripted sabbat. He perversely looks at the most uncharacteristic elements of the narrative, and thus neglects the story hidden in the heart of the sabbat fantasies of the Inquisition, and by extension, the folk, for unless these elements were familiar then the idea would not have taken root across Europe. It was in fact already deep within the black soil of cultural memory and practice. As a witch not tethered by my umbilical to the academy but wearing it with my caul around my neck, I can go further. Far from deciphering the sabbat, an impossibility in itself, Ginzburg has been used to deny us the power of the grand demonological sabbat and lead us on a flight in another direction. Tonight we will feast on children, maim, murder, fuck and frolic. What seems monstrous may simply be a trick of the moonlight, but this is where we must go.

My thesis is that the sabbat is the survival of the mystery cults and a resurrection mythology which is concealed in the Great Rite itself, the mystery within the mystery. I have a clear intent, and though I will cite Ginzburg, Wilby and Pócs, I want us to celebrate the sabbat again not by standing unsteadily on a stack of books, but on the sabbat mountain itself.

The difficulty for historians is that they are in a state of constant revision, picking over the testimony with each generation and using the methodology which is currently permitted by the academy. This will never transform and take them to the sabbat, and to be fair, that is not their aim. Historiography is not the realm of witchcraft at all. Furthermore, their history will never have the testimony of the beliefs of the poor, the peasants, the folk, those who keep silent, making it impossible to ever gain the objective view which history pretends to. The inner life is not written. History is as amorphous as any dream, the methods are simply attempts to grasp at its diaphanous dancing form without entering into the divine madness where knowledge truly resides.

This is not to dismiss the academic approach, simply put, it needs to have its place, which is not as arbiter or transmitter of myth. This is the role of the poet, the writer, the shaman, the witch. Neither is an academic approach necessarily inimical to witchcraft, something those who attack academics cannot grasp. They simply feel emotionally wounded due to the perceived assault on myth and its resulting disenchantment. They have failed to understand the transcendent power of symbols. So too have the disenchanters, so proud of their dissection that they forget to notice that the heart has long since ceased beating.

Let us take for example the work of Margaret Murray, whose misreading of the Inquisition's body count became canonised as 'nine million menstrual murders' by Penelope Shuttle and Peter Redgrove in *The Wise Wound*. When Murray wrote this an army of women responded, because they felt the continuity, the blood thread spun from their wombs. They felt the nine million menstrual murders being perpetrated by patriarchy and Redgrove, Shuttle and many others gave voice to that. They could see that culture was trying to destroy them, and projected this dream back into the past as an anti-Christian religious survival. The emotional truth created the myth from which it had been projected. Surely this should be celebrated as powerful witchcraft? The delight with which the Murray thesis has been tortured and consigned to the purifying flames by her inquisitors is a proof in itself of the power. You do not take such countermeasures against an impotent threat.

Jules Michelet is the other mythographer of note, whose revolutionary witchcraft remains a potent inspiration. Though the discrediting of the Étienne-Léon de Lamothe-Langon's *Histoire de l'Inquisition en France*, as his major source was an important academic acid wash, it does not dissolve the mythic base beneath. Michelet proposed an anti-Christian witch cult, and we proudly stand in that tradition of *non serviam*, of *I shall not lie beneath*. An avowedly anti- or, more accurately, post-Christian witchcraft does not need a lineal survival, or the foot-noted approval of anyone, because simply put it works, whether the French peasants gathered in nocturnal assemblies against the oppression of Church and state led by a sorceress, or not. I would argue that our very existence proves that we have ancestry.

Academics are horrified when they find discredited ideas still being used and repeated by witchcraft practitioners. They see sloppy research which should be corrected, but this is to completely fail to understand the mythic needs of the narrative, they ignore both the internecine squabbling within academia and the very spell woven by witchcraft itself. As a result here I will spare both the neopagan roll call of the latest transgressors and that father of lies, Robert Graves. I will also not get embroiled in the controversies of professional historians whose tenure is predicated on opening wounds. In describing the mythic sabbat I am also not privileging one tradition above another, and hope that this pool of moonlight which I stand in is not mistaken for the entire ocean of night.

So I choose to engage with the most discredited of myths, and yet the most archetypal, the sabbat, not in the redacted variant of Gardner or Ginzburg, or the oblique personal misprision of Kenneth Grant and Austin Osman Spare, but in the grand panorama of the height of the witch panic. The sabbat fully fledged and terrible to behold. I wish to step through into the deepest nocturnal secret with you all, because it is somewhere that I have trodden. There is veracity, truth, power and transformation to be found in this dance. When I present the myth as it has been revealed to me, it is to illuminate as surely as the torch rising between the horns of the sabbatic goat. Though there are initiated traditions, no group can control or monopolise the sabbat. It is not a trademark, it is an experience which is open to all. To do this we will follow the structure of the myth itself which will become increasingly riotous as the winds furl around the barren peak, dancers and devils begin to blur and merge as sharp faces stab into bold relief only to be lost once more.

Who is it that attends the sabbat but the witch? Thus modern discussions of who attends the sabbat are often dialogues of exclusion, where one group seeks to insist that they are the only true witches, that their experience is in some way more authentic than any other. Those who choose a solitary path either by inclination or circumstance are particularly vunerable to these unjustified attacks. But the sabbat is far more egalitarian than that, it strips away difference. It summons us. This calling is the inner aspect that defines a witch, rather than the outer social aspect of the accusatory pointed finger of condemnation. The first flight to the sabbat is very often a spontane-ous event. One which is not mediated by coven or ritual. It is a lucid, though often shocking, transfiguration.

Rather like the abduction narratives of fairy and saucer cults, those who are taken once tend to be taken again and again. I would tenta-tively suggest that it is only when you deliberately choose to return to the sabbat and be taught how to access it that you can be count-ed a witch. The often punctual arrangements made with the spirits or fairies or devils, is something we also see in John Dee's angelic conversations and the conventions of high magic where timing is a critical calibration. Flight then becomes chosen rather than coercion, you are a participant and not a victim. The witch herself masters the powers of flight whether by fairy whirlwind, sieve, stang or thighs clamped about the hoary besom. What I can say is that some are more susceptible to this than others, and that this sensitivity is recognisable as kin. We read the marks more surely than any Bible. What begins alone becomes a joined dreaming with those whom we coven with or encounter there, and so the conspiracy is born.

As witches we have been consistently labelled deluded, hysterical, sick or simply high. Sometimes that might be true. Whilst keeping our footing on the unsteady fantasia of the sabbat ground we should consider these critiques, as they may unwittingly provide us with fur-ther steps taking us from the periphery towards the centre the dance revolves around.

Johannes Wier and Reginald Scot with their rational explanation for witchcraft as the delusion of old women was not one welcomed by the clerical legal establishment who sought tinder that would crackle at the touch into hellfire and not boughs of green wood that would slowly smoke out the flame. Though Wier saved lives, this idea began the process of pathologising altered states, as trial records clearly show that those who were accused of witchcraft were not mentally ill or simple-minded. In an increasingly materialist world this idea prevailed but the focus shifted from the old women who kept an oral tradition alive and an enchanted view of the world, to the distempered ravishment of youth. The delusion was labelled hysteria under the psychoanalyst's probing. All the exponents of the *Malleus Maleficarum* now donned white coats and clipboards and bade our witch recline onto the clinician's couch. We find the resistance to this in Hélène Cixous and Catherine Clément's *The Newly Born Woman*, in which Clément writes:

> One must go through the audience of writers, psychiatrists, and judges to reconstitute the mythical stage on which women played their mythical role. The last figure, the hysteric, resumes and assumes the memories of the others: that was Michelet's hypothesis in *The Sorceress*; it was Freud's in *Studies on Hysteria*. Both thought that the repressed past survives in woman, woman more than anyone else, is dedicated to reminiscence. The Sorceress, who in the end is able to dream nature and therefore conceive it, incarnates the reinscription of the traces of paganism that triumphant Christianity repressed. The hysteric, whose body is transformed into a theatre for forgotten scenes, relives the past, bearing witness to a lost childhood that survives in suffering.

Witchcraft is not over. Clément insists: 'Somewhere every culture has an imaginary zone for what it excludes, and it is that zone we must try to remember today.' The sabbat is such a zone, such a remembering and this is why it must be the core practice of witchcraft, and one sought with some foreboding. Its forbidden aspects cannot be neatly excised unless we wish to wake in backless gowns sutured, sexless and staring out with blank eyes at a world that has lost its secret meanings. We will not have it driven out of us by electro-convulsive therapy, or flat-lined away with chemical constraints.

It is high time for us to set out for the sabbat. Let us look through the keyhole, the devil's perspective, and also the priest's, to where by candlelight the naked woman anoints her smooth limbs with the salve. We can be permitted this small act of voyeurism because witchcraft and ritual is erotic. We all wish to witness what is forbidden, or sacred, but we will have to participate to truly understand or suffer Actaeon's fate. Looking through the cottage door on our now sleeping witch, unless our hearts have been replaced with straw, we too can share her dreams that ascend as surely as the smoke which rises from the fire in the hearth.

Having discounted senility, hysteria, madness, is the secret of the witch in this sensual unguent, this deliberate action, this second expedition which follows the first spontaneous rapture?

Many have engaged in the futile search for soma, the missing entheogen or admixture that ravished women up in flight and carried them away to a sexual carousel of beautiful youths. There are accounts of this being a deep sleep, a narcolepsy, a catalepsy that reminds us in particular of amanita muscaria and the ecstasies of the Tunguskan shaman laid out as stiff as frozen hide. Somewhere we hear the slow muffled beat of the reindeer skin drum heart. Is it the drugs that allow us to find our way back to the rendezvous on the naked heath?

Herbs were indeed the *materia magica* of witchcraft in the ancient world, as Pliny states in his *Natural History* xxv:5:

Nothing else will be found that aroused greater wonder among the ancients than botany. Long ago was discovered a method of predicting eclipses of the sun and moon – not the day or night merely but the very hour. Yet there still exists among a great number of the common people an established conviction that these phenomena are due to the compelling power of charms and magic herbs, and that the science of them is the one outstanding province of women.

It was only with the Roman period that the use of herbs in witchcraft was replaced by the ghoulish use of the corpse, as the figure of the witch became demonised in the literary tradition. Can we argue then that herbal knowledge survived, and in particular the secrets of the flying ointments?

There are proofs. In *The Book of the Sacred Magic of Abramelin the Mage*, tentatively dated at 1458, the protagonist encounters a sorceress in Lintz who sensually rubs the pulses of his hands and feet with an unguent and leaves him convinced of the corporeality of the experience. However, when he asks her to repeat the experiment and travel for him to report back on a friend, he is dismayed to see her simply fall into a sleep for three deep hours:

> Whence I concluded that what she had just told me was a simple dream, and that this unguent was a causer of phantastic sleep; whereon she confessed to me that this unguent had been given to her by the Devil.

We will return the detail of the devil a little later, for now we should note the context: this adventure appears in a series of escapades with the 'wrong sorts' of magic before engaging in the *Abramelin* operation proper. It seems likely that though a morality tale of sorts, it is a repetition of folklore, and likely represents both popular understanding and, critically, practice. Della Porta, in his *Magia Naturalis* of 1558, records a similar experiment with a witch who applies the salve to herself and goes into a deep trance, during which he and his companions beat her, ostensibly to prove that she did not physically fly away. Della Porta gives a recipe for the ointment which is quickly suppressed, having garnered the opprobrium of the fanatical Jean Bodin, amongst others, for both challenging the corporeality of the sabbat and providing the wherewithal to attend one. For the record, Della Porta's salve is one of the few Neapolitan dishes I would not recommend sampling, containing as it does the active ingredients of monkshood and hemlock.

The use of medicinal and magical salves is a historical fact, and these salves will have contained the baneful witchcraft herbs. Their miraculous powers appear in the classics and in particular we can credit the account of Apuleius in *The Golden Ass* as an inspiration for this genre.

Having spied as Pamphile turns into an owl, Lucius greedily smears on the ointment:

> I stood, flapping my arms, one after the other, as I had seen Pamphile do, but no little feathers appeared upon them and they showed no sign of turning into wings. All that happened was that the hair on them grew coarser and coarser and the skin toughened into hide. Next, my fingers bunched together into a hard lump so that the five fingers on my hands became single hooves, the same change came over my feet and a long tail sprouted from the base of my spine. Then my face swelled, my mouth widened, my nostrils dilated, my lips hung down and my ears bristled long and hairy. The only consoling part of this miserable transformation was the enormous increase in the size of my member...

The misadventures of Apuleius confirm a long history of night flight, animal transformation, salves and sexual sorcery. We are a long way from a definitive recipe, but there are clearly elements of the sabbat here which are not simply the fantasies of the inquisition but are core witchcraft practices. The tale of Apuleius is indeed repeated as fact by Nicholas Rémy in his influential 1595 work *Demonolatry*. Apuleius also reminds us, as does Circe in her transformation of Odysseus' crew into swine, that there is a price to be paid for transgression. Pigs are the chthonic sacrifice par excellence in the ancient world. Witchcraft requires drugs, but the same preparation can make us swine or asses as readily as owls. This is one of the most important lessons, the drugs are not enough, we are an irreducible element in the equation.

As we saw from Della Porta, the herbs compounded into the salve are poisons. Extraction and toxicology are a major issue here. Experimentation must account for the dramatic variance in concentration of the alkaloids. This can be said of henbane, belladonna, mandrake, datura, hemlock, aconite and monkshood. This is not to discount the use of the poison plants in visionary experience as they do induce sensations of flying and erotic reveries. However, the idea that witchcraft is simply a drug cult is a profound misrepresentation. The theory that the flying ointments are simply lists of toxic worts has some truth. They are fundamentally plants of the dead, those that as pharmakon both heal and harm. It is this connection with the dead, and the places of the dead, that we keep close with us.

Given that sabbat flight and a very physical encounter with the devil precede the use of the salve, other explanations have been proposed. Some accounts have a Europe of poisoned peasants, famine driven to devour the wolf in the rye. Horned ergot baked in blighted bread is the rationalists attempt to dissolve the sabbat into a drugged muddle of regurgitated fairy tales and false memory. This seems an unlikely event given the difficulty of dosage and the lack of any reliable recipe or an attested tradition of ritual ergot use. The symptoms of ergotism were recognised, and not conflated with witchcraft. Starvation, deprivation and stress were however very real. It seems that this is one of the reasons for so many encounters with the other world that we in the West have forgotten. Fasting is a prerequisite for much magical work. Let us not neglect this, if we aspire to fly or to properly prepare ourselves for the ordeals of the visionary plants.

It has been suggested by entheogen enthusiasts that the reason that the narcotic salve was not pursued or criminalised in a proto war on drugs by the courts and Inquisitors in Europe is that they were intent on proving the physical existence of the sabbat and an actual, as opposed to an imaginal, criminal conspiracy. This position holds that the sabbat is given corporeality by the elites alone; therefore it argues the *Canon Episcopi* denial of the physical reality of the sabbat is the story we should cleave to. Yet the evidence of the trials tells a very different story. The Inquisitors changed their story as a result of the weight of testimony, not through closed and leading questions from accusation to auto-da-fé. It is what Emma Wilby styles *a dialectic between belief and experience*. Those who were accused insisted in the face of interrogation that their experiences were real. There is a further ecclesiastical bind, if the devil is corporeal, then the sabbat must be too.

Even De Lancre credited the drug suggestion, but broadens the net to include smokes, herbs, salves, and compares it to the New World insufflation of *cohoba* (better known as *yopo*, a DMT containing snuff). The borders of witchcraft even then were as permeable as any mucus membrane or fumbled customs search. He writes:

> Others have said, and not without making a great deal of sense, that the notorious female witches were first transported into an ecstatic state through the use of ointments, herbs, or fumigations that dulled their senses and, during their rapture, made them see all that took place at the sabbat, or something similar to the sabbat. This is just like the effect of the cohoba herb on the Indians in the island of Hispaniola. After a violent and troubled sleep, the Indians awaken and tell fantastic stories. Afterwards the Devil, having often shown them the sabbat in their dreams during their ravishments and ecstasies, leads them there very easily, both bodily and in reality and sometimes even keeps them in doubt as to whether this is an effect of illusion or the truth, so that they never know for sure.

De Lancre's tightrope allows for drugs giving a vision of the sabbat, but then an actual physical event occurring, which leaves it impossible for the witch to decipher which is real. This is a typical demonologist's trap that damns you whichever side of the line you fall.

What confounds us is the nature of the experience itself, which cannot be laboratory tested. There is no place for the observer once the witch has taken flight. It is occuring within and through the tumult of the body of the witch, and ultimately only she knows the truth. Is Della Porta's beaten body of the witch evidence? It is not. The sleeping body left behind is a counterfeit, a broom, a straw stuffed bundle.

Another particular difficulty is that the class of drugs listed in the salves destroys memory, confronts us with denizens of the other world seemingly as real as we are, and are generally hellish suffocating places for us to be. Navigation here is difficult, even for the seasoned traveller an almost insurmountable problem. This does not match the extensive testimony on the nature of the sabbat and encounters with denizens of the otherworld which are more often than not, bright, bright, bright. The details are exquisite, and the narrative not shot full of holes. I am not denying the worth of these compounds when applied sparingly, but would argue they are not where the secret solely resides. The salve in trial records is not simply a smearing of bear fat and henbane. It is almost always given to the witch by the devil who compounds it or potentialises it with his spit. This is a manifestly magical substance being prepared, a green alchemy if you will, that is more than the sum of its parts. It is a magical medicine not a polymer chain. The compound also requires incantation to potentialise it, the spoken (or better chanted) and sung charm which is what the saliva of the devil symbolises.

Before we leave the poisons behind, let us remember that these are poisons. Witchcraft is an art of going *and returning*, as anyone who has spent time in the mountains will understand. Focussing your gaze on the snowy peaks alone will get you killed, and not daring will never see you summit. The wise must balance these contradictory states. So here is a final paradox to consider: we do not need to necessarily poison ourselves to go the sabbat, but we do need to be dead. Other methods can be suggested here, whether ravished out of our bodies into post-coital trance, hung on hooks, rigged up in cradles or simply rocking in a chair, there is no one way to go other than wisely.

Does this all mean that Michelet was wrong when he intuited that great nocturnal gatherings took place? No. The sabbat, though dreamt, can also coincide with the body and with ritual, it is this that witchcraft should pursue with diligence and the precision of elf-shot. Even tangible states can be liminal, an experience that ritualists are well aware of. Time and reality are not the same in the circle or out in the woods. My considered position on whether the sabbat is physical or not is that the question itself is absurd. Witches do not divide the states of sleep and dream and vision. This magical monism is something rare in literate and partitioned modern minds. It is a shamanic conception that must be embodied in our witchcraft practice if it is to both have and provide meaning.

What is the salve actually for? What is the reason for all these lubricious witches? Gardner has a go at it; he tries the practical, keeping warm while naked, and follows it up with the improbable (though perhaps puckishly humorous) slipping out of the grip of the witch hunters, rather like a bar of soap in the bath. I choose to view ensalving as enabling us to slip between one state and another. By seeing it in this light, we can compare the preparation of the body for sabbat with the other three great rituals of purification, those of birth, marriage and death. Each of these is a ritual of annointing with a physical substance and an analogue, whether with amniotic fluid and holy water, sexual fluids and spikenard or myrrh and tears. These can be considered flying ointments. The sabbat is a mélange which contains all of these three rituals, with marriage as the knot that ties birth and death together. This is where the secret of the sabbat resides.

The salve has another purpose, hidden in the ingredient list. Not the baby fat suggested in the *Malleus Maleficarum* (which Redgrove intuits to be menstrual blood), but a more subtle one. It is often compounded with soot. A small detail, this is overlooked as not sensational or psychoactive enough, yet for me this small detail has been revelatory. One purpose of the salve with this ingredient is to blacken the face and limbs, just as Shiva is smeared with ash from the cremation ground. We are becoming dead, as spirits invisible to the living who cannot see us risen in the whirlwind. To be as no man, no one, to pass unchallenged in the bacchanal and spirit throng having erased our name among the living, we are now forever changed, at one with the fey and the dead. We are mummers, morris, beelzebus – burned black by the fierce sun of the grave, involved in something archaic yet vital.

But, back to Redgrove. As we encountered in 'The cup, the cross and the cave,' menstruation is a particularly feverish time of dreaming. A dark moon flight occurs, yet this is not the sabbat. Though if we accept the inclusion of menstrual blood in the salve, it gifts us with access to the dreaming depths at the very opposite point of the cycle. This is a particularly witchy trick. The recipe then includes a base of ash, blood and fat that may not be demonstrably traditional but is highly potentised. It is the *bindu* which links the eye above with the eye below; thus zenith and nadir coincide at the sabbat.

The nocturnal flight is bound to another important aspect, that of animal transformation. Again, this is a shamanic motif. I would opine that when we become or ride upon animals, it is because they are our ancestors, literally familiars. We are becoming the dead. Not in general, but in particular: our dead, our blood, our totem. Other familiar objects are pressed into service as mounts, very much a fairy motif, but the power of flight is also given by the devil, a nuanced term here, which covers a multitude of spirited creatures as it always has.

This transformation in turn requires another vital element, the weeping blood, milk and dew heavy moon. So now we have the delicate issue of timing. When is it that the sabbat takes place? It seems impossible not to conclude that the sabbat occurs on the full moon. This is critical to our understanding of the whole mechanism of myth. Once more, the trial records bear this out, with Isobel Gowdie attending *at each change of the moon,* though in the fevered writing of De Lancre the sabbat occurs nightly; this is clearly an exaggeration. This seemingly simple observation leads us to a remarkable conclusion, that the whole idea of the sabbat was not simply part of a slur on the Jews which was then transferred onto the witches during the contagion of the Inquisition, but is part of an older lunar tradition and calendar. It is both a memory and a survival, though along a path more crooked than linear. The full moon is the night of celebration, it is not the only night when witchcraft takes place, but it is the only candidate for the convening of the sabbat.

Sabbat itself is not a word derived from the Hebrew, it entered the lexicon via the Canaanites who had in turn inherited it from Babylon and the Sumerian *šabattu*. The word can be dissected joint by joint, *ša-bat-tu* or heart-rest-day, and was celebrated on the fifteenth day of each month. Fifteen is an encoded name of the goddess because of the time it signifies: not the coming of menstrual blood but her full risen potency. The fifteenth is the day of Inanna's descent to the underworld, but more on that later. It is also the numeration of the tarot trump The Devil whom, as I have proposed, is an image of the goddess concealed. All this is important to us, as Inanna is the origin of the demonised goddesses whom the Bible calls whore, and whom our rites are performed beneath. This fifteen is reinforced by another number important in witchcraft, thirteen, the number of full moons in a lunar year and the full complement of the traditional coven needed to perform this ritual. On such moonbeams, our tradition can be said to extend from the very cradle of civilisation, not always mouth to ear, but blood to blood.

So the witches rise like slender straws from the threshing floors held in invisible eddies and dust motes. Where is it that they are going?

Scripture reveals that Christ attends a sabbat himself and deports himself most ungraciously. In Matthew IV we read how, after fasting for forty days and forty nights in the wilderness, he encounters the devil. The devil challenges him to turn stones into bread. We see the devil and the fairy folk often do likewise, turning stones into bread and coins, as well as providing the sabbat banquet or fairy feast that we will sample in due course. Christ does not deign to do so. He is not that sort of wonder worker. He is then physically transported to the pinnacle of the Temple and tempted to jump that the angels might catch him. He refuses to demonstrate the power of flight with the aid of spirits, a spectacle which Simon Magus and other god-men of his age were more than happy to show. The scene changes once more:

Again, the devil taketh him up into an exceeding high mountain, and sheweth him all the kingdoms of the world, and the glory of

96

them; And saith unto him: All these things will I give thee, if thou wilt fall down and worship me.

This is the offering of pact. Note, as the Inquisition did, that the devil gives him the power of flight. Surely this is the sabbat, celebrated at the high place we are warned off with such consistency in the Bible. There is power and meaning here that Christ is scorning in an attempt to differentiate himself from other magicians. Another clue is concealed in the forty days of fasting; forty is a Venus number and associated with the kingship rite and necromantic resurrection that this cult sought to hijack as Judaism has done since Moses the murderer fled Egypt. The irony is that this is exactly what the witches' sabbat preserves.

But we do not need either the Prince of the Powers of the Air in such a redacted form, nor a reticent Messiah. The winds that carry us, raise us in swirls and streams to the sabbat, on whatever cleft stick or contrivance, are the dead, the ancestors as Wild Hunt driven by the scorpion-tipped whip of the goddess who goads lions around the Sumerian zodiac and whose high places once smoked with incense. We are journeying in our transformed bodies to a singular destination, the sacred mountain. This is the vision of the Grand Sabbat. The participants come from the flung compass points, there is no uniformity, but quite the opposite, all heresies are on the wing.

To name this place we need to borrow a word, as there is none in our lexicon that describes the coinciding state that marks out such a fairy mound. We call this as the Mesopotamians did, the *kur*, which is at once both peak and underworld, a physical mountain range and a designator of the foreign place. Death is always the other country.

The sabbat is celebrated on the mountain, the hollow hill. It is literally a topos, both a place and an endlessly repeated mythic motif. Many feet have stood on the same mountain, which in one sense is the primordial mound risen from the chaos of the waters. When we dance upon it we become part of this great cycle. This is the mythic mountain that the Sun descended within every night in the *Epic of*

Gilgamesh, and still does. The way is guarded by scorpions, a sign of the constellation that rises to mark the imminent death of the Sun at the Winter solstice. It is also the place where all life arises. The mountain is therefore where we resolve the lunar and solar calendars the 12 by 13 that could be described as the union of magician and witch, woman and beast, goddess and god. The sun which dies and is reborn and the moon which waxes and wanes renewing itself.

In the *Epic of Gilgamesh,* Enkidu describes the underworld as revealed to him in dream and it has strikingly sabbatic components. First comes animal transformation and flight, then follows the entry into the mountain and the feasting of the dead. Here as in the medieval Feast of Asses, kings serve their servants, all is topsy-turvy in the world below. The text fragments still crackle:

> I stood (alo)ne. His face was darkened. Like unto (...) was his face. (like)the talons of an eagle were his claws. (...) he overpowered me.(...) he leaps. (...) he submerged me. {mutilated or missing} (...) he transformed me, so that my arms were (...) like those of a bird. Looking at me, he leads me to the House of Darkness, the abode of Irkalla, to the house which none leave who have entered it, on the road from which there is no way back, to the house wherein the dwellers are bereft of light, where dust is their fare and clay their food. They are clothed like birds, with wings for garments, and see no light, residing in darkness. In the House of Dust, which I entered, I looked at (rulers), their crowns put away; I (saw princes), those (born to) the crown, who had ruled the land from the days of yore. (These doubl)es... of Anu and Enlil were serving meat roasts; they were serving baked meats and pouring cool water from the waterskins. In the House of Dust, which I entered, reside High Priest and acolyte, reside incantatory and ecstatic, reside the laver-anointers of the great gods, resides Etana, resides Sumuqan, Ereshkigal (lives there), Queen of the Netherworld.

The *kur* is where the Gods convene, and where they are entombed. Within the mountain the ancestors are buried, and the children are hidden away.

Another form of the hollow mountain is the human skull and another form of the human skull is the rose. In Siddha tradition the cosmic mountain is the body of the meditating initiate, the cave the cranium, the dancing ground the pate or crown. In our witchcraft the veneration of the skull as ancestor is an exteriorisation of what can then become an interior transformation. Thus the skull contemplation can be used to access the mysteries of the sabbat. David Gordon White observes: 'the Siddha universe was so constructed as to enable the practitioner to simultaneously experience it as a world in which he lived, and a world that lived within himself.' Surely this is the sabbat as described by the medieval witches who claimed to attend in bodily form? This may not simply be magical flight, but the path to apotheosis and power.

The mountain is also the enchanted castle, it is the seven stepped ziggurat with its bridal chamber cave, it is the tower and its princess beneath a lightning streaked sky. It is Kailash, Blocksberg, Pendle Hill. For the purposes of witchcraft we do not need any more than our bare feet kissing the earth, as we are bound to the very first moment, the first ritual celebration we made. This for us is the naked form of the sabbat, it is something shared, somewhere that we can all agree to meet.

The magician pauses and asks *to what end?* This can be answered by a further question: What is it that occurs at the sabbat ground? It seems a lot of effort for a mere orgy. De Lancre acknowledges the diversity of the sabbat, but points out that in spite of this the most serious ceremonies are consistent. I will do likewise and consider the themes of dismemberment, feasting, dancing and fucking.

The experience of the sabbat often involves dismemberment. Here the hero is cut up and placed in the cauldron. This is a universal shamanic symbol of initiation and is a dream many of us will have had before encountering the extensive anthropological literature. It is not a pleasant experience. The initiate is often seized by a flying creature and torn by talons and beak, this is what we saw in the *Epic of Gilgamesh* and what we find at the origins of Tantra or in the myths of Osiris, Tammuz, Dionysos or the Bull of the Heavens. We are sacrificed. The body is then reconstituted, often in a pot, though implanted with a secret bone, stone, element or shod with metal, or perhaps we are gifted it as an external talisman and power source.

Mircea Eliade, in his classic *Shamanism: Archaic Techniques of Ecstasy*, describes the three great mythico-ritual themes of dismemberment, ascent to the sky and descent to the underworld adding: 'but it should not be forgotten that such a separation rarely corresponds to the reality…the three chief initiatory themes sometimes coexist in the experience of the same individual; and that, in any event they are usually found together in any one religion.' This is exactly what we find in witchcraft. Three as one. The cauldron is womb, cave, underworld, mountain and sabbat itself. The turning of the dancers is the stirring of the pot. *Katabasis* and *anabasis* are simultaneously contained at midnight on the mountain. But before we congratulate ourselves on being part of a shamanic continuum, we must let Eliade conclude his quote:

> Finally it should be borne in mind that these ecstatic experiences, while they constitute the experience proper, always form part of a complex system of traditional instruction.

However you wish to cut it, this is not the case in the West. There is no evidence for the survival of a complex system, we are the inheritors of splintered bones, toppled crosses, and violated grave mounds. Our task is only beginning, though it would be more lucrative and reassuring to claim otherwise. Scraps of folklore need to be underpinned by a complete set of bones or they are simply rags blowing in the wind. Yet perhaps the sabbat itself is the key to re-establishing our cults. We must be honest about this, and acknowledge the debt we owe to the living traditions that are helping us reanimate our own.

The dismemberment and being feasted upon is followed by the feast itself. There are two variants here with one common origin. First is the fairy feast, which has a benign quality to it. This has been suggested as the fantasy of a peasant class who in starvation told tales of plenty and dreamt of being feasted in the fairy court. Let me briefly say that this is too simplistic. There are also benefic traditions of the spirit host passing through houses, eating without diminishing the food and giving the hosts prosperity. The second kind is the macabre witches' feast of raw flesh. This is an archaic element and one we find in Euripides' *Cretans*, where the leader of the chorus affirms: 'after celebrating the thunder of night roaming Zagreus (Dionysos Chthonios) and the raw feast, and holding up the torches for the Mountain Mother, and being consecrated in the armed dances of the Kouretes, I received the title of bacchos.' The raw flesh here is the dismembered animal, the same as the one taken down by the wild bacchantes. The celebrants are not human, but neither are they animals, they are something more than this. There seems little difference between this and the Wild Hunt, Fairy Horde or gaggle of witches who fly by night and kill cattle. Often these animals are resurrected by wrapping the bones in the hides and die later from what seems to be natural causes. This does perhaps reveal a palaeolithic strata to the whole sabbat construct, where the death of the animals in hunting is mediated between the shaman and the Mistress of Beasts. As the sabbat is where we meet and feast our ancestors, we should not be surprised when some prove to be very old indeed.

In the case of witches, the raw flesh in particular is that of innocent babes. Of all the images of the sabbat this remains the most troubling. It would be easy to dismiss it as black propaganda, but we need to dwell on this ghoulish image. The sabbat reflects an age of high infant mortality and seemingly random death. Witchcraft was the mechanism by which this was understood, as shamanism puts it: there is no such thing as a natural death. Witches, whether they kill by elf-shot, curse doll or giving the eye are part of the ecology of the cosmos. This has always been part of the function of the shaman, and one that sits uncomfortably with the community. Those who heal can harm, Cecil Williamson himself described witches as murderers. In many cultures there is a mechanism by which the killers are absolved of responsibility; they are acting as Fates, Valkyries, or in the manner of the Corsican *mazzeri*. This role as fate for us is presided over by Babalon whose cup contains the blood of all living things and the draught of which gives knowledge. Personally motivated malefica is better performed at the dark moon. Yet witches may find themselves acted against by the community if they are seen as persistently unjust.

If we eat of the animals and grains, the children of our mother, then something is required in recompense. Without death there is no life. The goddess devours her children, she is the black sow. In partaking of the sabbat you are undifferentiated from her. In this act, you are the goddess. In our practice the children are the red honey, the menstrual blood that is the key to the hollow hill both tasted and daubed upon our bodies in the salve, thus we are the children we incestuously devour and they are our parents and progeny. Thus the moment of the full moon sabbat is a totality which contains the dark moon within it. This cannibalistic orgy is nature herself. In *The Red Goddess*, I allude to a vision that I had of everything fucking everything, well, let me revise that, the sabbat is everything eating and fucking everything.

Another reason for the feast is that the dead are hungry, the dead are thirsty, the dead are cold. It is imperative that we provide for them as we will stand amongst them all too soon. It would be wise to have friends among the dead when you arrive. As witches we do not eat the dead, we care for their bones, this is the origin of necromancy, as much as taking the bones from condemned men we have laid them out in our barrows, we have exhumed them and washed them with our tears, we have sung to them. What marks us out as a culture with no future is that we do not do this. By feasting as and among the dead we let them partake of what they loved in life. There is a further reason, the chain of ancestry is maintained and our link to the dead who will be reborn as their ancestors in turn but will also aid us in the afterlife. These are the great lines and lineages of spirits and the mystery of reincarnation.

The furious energy of the dead manifests in a dance of a strikingly erotic character; this is a description of the archaic rites of ecstacy overwritten with the prurient sensibilities of whatever current age of prohibition holds sway. As I write this, Islamic fundamentalists in North Africa have announced a ban on music and dancing, but such an act is doomed to failure. The sabbat will not be denied. The demonisation of music and dance is the hallmark of a repressive culture and the inevitable tumescent riotous reaction to it. Dance is a form of resistance to the socialised body, whether the de-sexualised automata of industrial culture parodied back as Detroit techno, or the writhing of nuns celebrating a new covenant with the flesh, or the dancing mania that invaded the churchyards, or the followers of Dionysos and Cybele going majnoon to the cymbals and flute. It is the irrepressible fire that sweeps through the marrow of the bones and articulates them again. It speaks, it raves. Dance is maximum extension, just as death is maximum contraction, the interplay between these states is the immortal moment of the dancing ground.

The demonologists wrote extensively on this, and none was more horrified than De Lancre. It is not merely the folk dances that betoken a pagan survival, but new forms of foreign lasciviousness that flood into a chaste culture. De Lancre blames the Basques, and in doing so his own denied ancestry:

> all the most excitable dances, and those that torment the body the most, those which disfigure it the most, and all the most indecent dances come from there. All the Pyrrhonic, the Moorish, the perilous jumps, dances on ropes, the cascading from high ladders, the flying with fake wings, pirouettes, the dancing on half lances, swinging, making circles, the forces of Hercules on the woman turned upside down without touching her back on the floor, (...) almost all these atrocities came from Spain.

He goes on to castigate the Saraband as the latest and most violent and passionate of all dances. Yet De Lancre is dead, and the Basques continue to dance and celebrate their witchcraft heritage.

The indiscriminate incest proposed by De Lancre with endlessly changing dancing partners differs from the account of Francesco Maria Guazzo in his *Compendium Maleficarum* of 1628, where it is the familiar spirit, a dæmon, with whom the witch cavorts:

> Each demon takes by his hand the disciple under his guardianship, and all the rites are performed with the utmost absurdity in a frenzied ring with hands joined and back to back; and so they dance, throwing their heads like frantic folk.

Interestingly, this head throwing is also seen in the mænadic dance of ancient Greece. The backward facing element is one in a series of inversions that Guazzo details both representing the classical depiction of the three Fates, and the aspect of anonymity which is so much a part of the sabbat and other banned folk practices such as guising. Witches attending the sabbat are likewise described as masked, disguised and veiled by Nicholas Rémy whom Guazzo relies upon in his descriptions, though omitting the former's note that they circle to the left, that is, widdershins, as the 'Druid priests' did.

Rémy adds one further aside: that witches were called *masca*, masks, by the Lombards and this is the root of the carnival celebration of masquerade, surely a form of the sabbat itself. The etymology of *mask* intrigues with its chain of associations and accords. Infiltrating our vocabulary via medieval Latin *masca* which evocatively signified a nocturnal female spectre, or a nightmare, or the mask by which the spectre was evoked; it was equated with the *striga*, *larva* and *lamia*. It is a word whose genealogy is obscure and manifold. A disputed etymology derives *masca* from the Arabic *maskharah*, a buffoon, whose root *sakhira* means to laugh, mock or ridicule. The Jewish Aramaic *mesaqqer*, to dye or paint red, has also been proposed, connected as it is with face painting during the Purim masquerade, celebrated on the 15th of the month of Adar in Jerusalem: 'the lustful daughters of Zion used to paint their eyes red.' Or perhaps Occitan *mascarar* and Old French *mascurer,* to darken, or blacken the face; and there is the Old Occitan *masco,* a witch or sorceress, whose roots may draw from a pre-Indo-European language. The word *mascotte* is related, being the witch's charm, talisman or fetich. And I find it curious that this root, of such an ancient and mixed lineage abides still in senses all convergent on the guised witch, her nocturnal art and the masque of living and dead souls.

Dance requires music and this too is seen as infernal, with pipers condemned in Scotland, the gypsy violin in Spain, the drum and the crazy flute in the ancient world and then of course jazz, rock and roll and repetitive beats. All are given mind altering seductive powers. The devil is still said to have the best tunes and these are an essential part of the celebration of the sabbat. We should all dance more and express our carnality. Rémy reports that:

> all is done to a marvellous medley and confusion of noises, and it is beyond the power of words to describe the uncouth, absurd and discordant sounds that are uttered there. For one sings to a pipe, or rather picks a rod or stick from the ground and blows upon it as if it were a pipe; another beats and strums with his fingers upon a horse's skull for a lyre, another beats an oak tree with a cudgel or heavy club, and so produces a roaring sound like the beating of heavy drums; and all the while the Demons sing with a raucous, trumpet-like voice, and the whole mob with roaring and harsh cries make the heavens echo and frenziedly rage, shouting, hissing and yelling.

At the sabbat, this is a sacred offering and the music is now reaching a crescendo. What is happening at the sabbat is an inversion; not simply upside down crucifixes or the moon language that the demonologists grappled with, but a literal inversion of earth and sky upon the vertical axis of the holy mountain beneath which the sun resides in his cavern and over which the full moon rises and casts forth her spectral light on the dancers. Midnight on the mountain is a peculiar time and one we must orientate ourselves in as the circle of masks whirls ever faster and our grip tightens and our feet begin to fly. Behind us the mystery itself is taking place. The union of goddess and king, witch and devil.

The outward facing masks of the dancers are apotropaic, they are Gorgon, Hekate, the spider, the spinner, the menstruating monster with bloody extended tongue. Their role is as guards and wards, the 64 dakinis arrayed in a mandala about the shiva-lingam are for us the thirteen moon maidens of coven. This wheeling circle of protective and baleful eyes is stronger than Cherubim or Merkavah. It throws out weird shadows, nightmares, flickering erotic impossibilities. It guards the thrones that are now invisible to the particpants whose silence is absolute on the matter because they cannot have witnessed the mystery.

The sabbat is both a banquet and a bridal bed. It is here that the Great Rite is celebrated. There is a striking parallel with Kaula Tantra, a medieval Indian expression of the self-same mysteries, and that like the Sabbat preserves a far older memory. This defines the form of witchcraft which we practice, but not every form of witchcraft. I defer to David Gordon White:

On certain nights of the lunar month and solar year, Kaula practitioners would assemble on cremation grounds, or clan 'mounds' or 'seats,' 'clan mountains' or 'fields.' These gatherings, called minglings, involved the union of female and male initiates, of Yoginis whose presence and interaction with their heroic or perfected male counterparts were the sine qua non of Kaula practice.

At these gatherings the Yoginis would descend from the sky to meet their male consorts awaiting them on the ground. These Yoginis flight' was fuelled by the human and animal flesh that was their diet; however the Siddhas or Viras by virtue of their own practice, were able to offer the Yoginis a more subtle and powerful energy source. This was their semen, the distilled essence of their own bodily constituents. The Yoginis, gratified by such offerings, would offer their form of grace to the Siddhas or Viras. Instead of devouring them, they would offer them a counterpresentation of their own sexual discharge, something these male partners would have been as needful of as the Yoginis were of male semen.

We do not need to be initiated Kaula tantrics when we have the same practices enshrined in the Witches' Sabbat and in the taboos and techniques of our own culture. This feast of nectar is a form of the sabbat, a mutual insanguination. We can go further – the flying yoginis are our strix. The Siddhas travelled to us as Dionysos who is both hero, Hades and, ultimately, devil.

The sabbat mount has by magic become the underworld. The underworld itself is vivified by the Sun as surely as the beam of Solstice dawn, heralded by Venus, penetrates the necropolis of New Grange. These events are simultaneous. This is more than a pair of dyads, it is a concresence, a coinciding, a cross-matching in the cauldron and crucible. From the interpenetration of the elements is born both death and life.

We can glyph this with the mythic protagonists of Father, Mother, Son and Daughter, and their counter-change in the seasons which brings forth new life. When the daughter is ravished into the underworld in the Spring she is joined to the Eld Father. This is the bearded goat, that is the Old Devil, mated to the virgin witch. But the sabbat is celebrated at midnight, and this means that the Sun, as the youthful god, has penetrated the underworld and is joined with the Mother. Thus as god and goddess celebrate on the mountain they mirror the union beneath. Green is to white, black is to red. This substitution and balance is the immutable law and justice of the underworld. It is a resurrection ritual, not of the body, but of the souls of the dead, the ancestors. In truth, there is no father, son, mother, daughter, but a unity on the immortal lightning crowned Venus mountain.

What is often forgotten in celebrating the golden sperm of the sun is that the moon gives forth nocturnal dew. Plutarch in his *Moralia*, citing Castor, notes that the dead souls live on the moon, whilst the body is resolved into the earth. The moon also sows new souls into the earth as it passes overhead. An image of this is contained in the tarot. It is the moon that brings the rains, and rain is our ancestor as it awakens the sleeping seeds in their tombs. At the sabbat this dew fall is provoked by erotic phrensy. In Thessalian witchcraft it is the witches who draw down the moon and for this they must be naked. The purpose of this rite is omitted in modern pagan witch-craft, namely to milk it of its dew. Lucan's Erictho famously does this for necromantic purposes. Yet this is how the dead are reborn, not simply in the crops but in human bodies who are the celebrants at the sabbat. This is the Great Rite and the central secret of witchcraft. I hope that we will all dance this way, in the bones of our ancestors.

VII

Midnight sun
Cut lustre
On jeweller's night
Draws us
Gather sabbatic
Bring grievances
Her witch eye
Sniper-sighted
Destroys
Block by block
The beautiful one
Stalks palaces and slums

A wolf sent forth
to snatch away a lamb

Have we forgotten how to hunger? Witchcraft has not, standing as it does in the thin line between the diminishing wild and a civilisation devouring itself. The bones stand out on us, a rolling loping dirty fur offering a red flower for a mouth. We do not expect to be under-stood, or welcomed by the herd or at the hearth. We have our own company to keep, our own loves and customs. Ours is the clamped tenacity that bears down the antler crowns of kings. Our desire, a glowing stolen coal of a heart.

We must be hungry for this knowledge. The hunger that ravens and slams against the cage of bone and wind, that scents blood through the crazed labyrinth of silver birch. We must leave if we are to return rather than mock snarl behind the muzzle of our social selves, to imagine as wolf and never feel that engine of raw need that sharpens us into other worlds and ghosts across the endless tundra of exile. In essence we must become rewilded.

Wolf pads beside the history of witch, now leopard, now lion. Moccasin soft tread. The meaning is very simple, even when the skin switches. It is one that has seen us hung from fences alongside the tattered crows: We all eat human flesh. Raw. We are vilified, shadows thrown by fear around the campfire.

But that is their story, the one which does not include the slaughter of the herds, the fences, the starvation wrought by the ploughshare, the view in on the worsening ways of man. They made us into this, and we are to be blamed for it, expected to melt away like frost. But we have already been pared down to the essential matter. Nomads and hunters have no burden, they simply move, but now there is nowhere left to go, no prey but them. Still we go on.

When the vexed question is raised about the role of men in witchcraft then the answer has already been given in the song of the wolf. Men are excluded from many of the rites of witchcraft. Men do not menstruate. Thus our mysteries differ from those of women. The warrior cults and kings were suckled by the supine bitch and weaned onto blood and battle, thirsty as cracked wine flasks. In one of the earliest accounts of witchcraft, Nider's 1437 *Formicarius* male witches are said to transform themselves into wolves. But we must not forget that women also become wolves. Lupa they call the prostitute and courtesans of Imperial Rome, Lupanar, the reek of the brothel. The wanting ones, the lying in wait, the insatiable panting jaws flecked with spittle.

To become a wolf is not for madmen only, so here we will not dwell on the murderers and psychotics of historical record whether Peter Stumpf or imagined Harry Haller. Nor will we valorise the lone individual, the damaged result of an atomising culture, but instead we will see the wolf within the sphere of the world. In order to do this we must see how the figures of wolf and witch and outlaw and warrior entwined. The wolf has too often been rune-hooked into a totem that the wolf itself would not recognise. This supposed wolf is set to devour the emotional self, the implied weakness, the feminine. We do not make such an elementary mistake in our witchcraft, as we view nature as she is, not as a projection of our own disintegrated failure to be complete. The wolf finds its own family.

Perhaps here we can include the work of Francis Bacon, the great marbled mottled flesh and dislocating jaws. The mouth, always painting the mouth which he found so beautiful. This quality of *vo-*

lupté which is both wolfish and luxuriating in the body enables us to rediscover our own bodies. Not the polite bodies of society, but the brutal collisions, the view through the bottom of the pint glass. The papal nuncios are always wolves, the popes too in their secret den, a city within Roma herself, just as Soho is a city within London. The queers and artists always creating mythical cities within themselves, having slunk long enough in the shadows, in their own society they wear their furs with justified pride. I interject these images because the words alone are never enough. We need the indecency of wet paint, conspiracy and instinctual actions. From the broken slashed canvases the wolves emerge.

The wolf eats children and maidens, and the most prevalent victims of the witches feast are also such innocents. Just as the night flying witches hurl their darts and kill the weak, the cattle, the crops, the prowling wolf plays a role in a continuous cycle of living and dying. It is not horror, but honesty that the red form of the goddess reveals to us in the sanctuary and grove. Attaching the wolf as an emblem to the abduction, murder and rape of children does not describe the actions of the animal. This is not a behaviour pattern which displays anything other than insanity, not any kind of cyclical action but a fracturing of natural relationships. The lone wolf is sick. Just as the witch as shaman accounts for all deaths within a community so too does the wolf and this in particular means accounting for infant mortality and those of the disappeared who do not make it to fairyland.

The cave is witness, the rock art, the stamped dances. We have been animals for longer than we have been men, and none more than that liminal disputed figure of shaman. The skin switches, hyena, lion, tiger, cat, hare, bull, bear and wolf. The animal which is not an animal. The man who is not a man. The witch who stands as intercessor between the hunters and the Mistress of the Beasts, who was the Mistress of the Beasts. It is her with whom we run.

It is the wolf that taught us how to hunt, the strategies of pack and drive and ambush and lure. The *metis* which is no longer recognised as the essential quality to cultivate is embedded in the shape of the wolf. They know the whetstone emptiness sharpening of sense. The predators are animals which plan and deceive like we do, whose forward facing eyes are calibrated as gun sights, ghosts who take the bait and leave the deadfall standing. Ghosts whom we have taken into our bones as ancestors. Mighty hunters who sing to their mother moon. They are also the mother and the hearth, the founders of civilisation and cities. Just as birds taught us language, wolf taught, teaches.

We must sweat the taint of civilisation out of us, empty our bellies, discard our human clothes. Rediscover need in the bath-houses and backstreets. Nudity means more than removing our clothes, and this must be fully accomplished for us to begin to trade one skin for the other. In a 17th century BCE Hittite text, wolf pelts give magical powers, but this has gone on longer. We partition their powers. Our knives have the same curve as their teeth. We necklace ourselves with them, wear their flayed masks, become them. They enable us to slip into the underworld, invisible. Coyote tails salvaged from road kill follow us. But as this happens wolves vanish from the wild, and we lose them from our chain of ancestors. It is only through witchcraft, not vivisection, that we can keep this connection alive, turn our coats inside out. The last bare tuft of tail becomes a love spell, and a potent one at that, but when the last wolf dies, so soon will the sterile herds. The wolf is a creature whose form we still take in dance and dream as the image of the Northern winter sun. The downed stag is the Summer king at bay. The men who go forth as wolves are the retinue of the divine huntress, a reckoning at large in the land, a stormy night that beckons to the bold whilst the dogs lie sleeping in their beds.

Here we are again at the sable and argent field of the sabbat, as worn and familiar as the old coin in the heavens. The wolves are both the spirits of the dead and the ancestors. That is, warriors and heroes; they are the transformed witches and the agency of the goddess herself. They are engaged in a hunt, that is, the exacting of nocturnal vengeance and restitution. There is both guising and sexual voracity, physical transformation, ritual action and the sending forth of the fetch. As we will later encounter there is also the salve, enchantment and eating of raw human flesh. All this occurs beneath the watchful eye of the full moon. It is the same familiar unfamiliar territory.

It seems the wolf as man is a proto-Indo-European idea, ranging into Slavic, Baltic and Germanic traditions. A warrior's mask, whose ferocity is praised in this specific ritualised context where the hunt has a particular quarry. It is as wolves that we are absolved and able to kill our own kind; we belong to another tribe. More pasture, more animals meant every young man had to raid and so Indo-European warriors were initiated in wolf skins, and the sign of the initiate was the magical (no doubt wolf skin) belt. This would have bestowed invulnerability and other magical powers upon the wearer. One belt was worn by the captain of the pack and two by the initiates showing their binding to both the ancestors and their allotted leader. A drilled tooth was rawhide-strung around their necks and they went naked besides that. In this way Korios, the warrior brotherhood mandated by the heavens, went ravening abroad. They have melted into our flesh as even their herds have sputtered into tallow, hides gone to tatters, bones broken and sucked clean of marrow. It must be remembered that we hold this book with their wolfish hands, look upon it from beneath their brow ridges, still use their words as the axle around which wheels our song.

The belt survived in Teutonic folklore where it becomes an explicitly magical ligature. In the account given by Wuttke in his *German Folklore*, a wolf or human skin belt, particularly that of a hanged man is fashioned and inscribed with the zodiac and affects the change. The magical belt is also notable in the grimoire tradition where a lion skin belt is worn by the Solomonic mage, but the transformation is by this stage neither explicit nor the aim of the rite, it is an implicit power that we do not harness, tethered instead to our learning and language. It is a decadent affectation.

Richard Verstegan in his 1605 *A Restitution of Decayed Intelligence in Antiquity*, (cited by Montague Summers) writes:

The werewolves are certain sorcerors, who having anointed their bodies with an ointment, which they make by the instinct of the devil, and putting on a certain enchanted girdle, do not only unto the view of others seem as wolves, but to their own thinking have both the shape and nature of wolves so long as they wear the said girdle.

This account is given to demonstrate continuity, the warrior has become part of the sorcerous conspiracy, the mistress of the beasts become the devil. We are simply another notch tighter than before, straining to breathe, we pant.

The girdle, belt or garter continues to be employed in witchcraft with more direct intent. If we are to undergo this shift then the belt is perhaps the one ritual item which must be made. The belt is also not without martial purpose, as it not only carries weapons, but it is the garb of a wrestler. The sacred nature of wrestling is often overlooked but in a warrior tradition is a critical test of strength. The belt is the minimum requirement to execute hip throws and holds whilst helping to support the lower back. This form of fighting requires a degree of intimacy and a relinquishment of personal space and ego which can be considered a form of magical training. Men should wrestle, need more wolf work than desk work, factory work.

The wolf-coat berserkers of the sagas show a continuity between bear and wolf which we also find in ancient Greece where the bear is called *bee-wolf*. This warrior cult was linked to the use of a magical potion, perhaps amanita muscaria, and the divine possession of frenzy. What moderns do not want to hear is that war is simply a special kind of hunt and that this is the male parallel to the menstruation of women, the thirsty spears and sword tongues are wet with a continuity of blood which flows from the sacred cave as it does from the animals whether two or four legged. That war is frenzy and that the soldiers are already dead, they belong to the goddess, whose desire as she-wolf they can never hope to match. She is the mistress of these blooded beasts, at home amongst the slaughter. She favours the brave and it is only they who will return to run with her as wolves on full moon nights. The initiatory cults of soldiery kept the mystery school understanding of the initiate and the first teaching of those who become shaman: you are already dead. This abandonment is the lesson of battle. The wolf is a Homeric simile for the advancing line and in modern war that line has become a circular jaw within which there are now no civilians left, just meat. We have been given no choice but to pick up the despised skin.

Both outlaws and warriors have long been characterised as wolves. In the sixth century Germanic and Norse law codes the term *warg* was a synonym for *outlaw*. Anglo-Saxon law stated that both outlaws and wolves should be killed on sight. Even the outlaw in the thirteenth century was described as having *a wolf's head* which could be cut off with impunity. The ancestor has become vermin, less than the enslaved and de-horned herd, but paradoxically grown more monstrous and voracious even as it dwindles away. A devil glimpsed at the edge of the village, crouched over a kill as traffic hisses by. When we write of becoming the wolf, we should not expect to receive a welcome. We are the risen carcasses and skin of the slain. Invoking them we clatter their iron bones and bells that sound off like stray rounds.

Pursuing our wolf, now down from the steppes and back through the black pine forests of Europe leads us to Greece and an oral tradition becoming a literary one. No longer are we relying on the enigmatic paintings of the artists who removed their finger joints and spat paint over them to leave the flash print signatures (this missing finger is preserved as a holy relic in the wounded werewolf fairytales, a bandaged paw). We are not interpreting a silhouette of a costume lost, a song's long echo. Yet the figure they venerated has survived here. Before Apollo there stands the she-wolf, a goddess down to her very ankles, a shapely bone sliver inserted even into the sheets of the Magical Papyri. She is the wolf-tamer, the mistress who is Queen amongst the predators. Homer preserves this in his description of the witch, or more properly goddess, Circe in Book X of the *Odyssey*:

They found Circe's house of polished stone, in a clearing in the forest glades. Round it wolves and mountain lions prowled, bewitched by Circe with her magic drugs. Instead of rushing to attack my men, they rose on their hind legs and wagged their tails. Like dogs fawning round their master, back from a feast, bringing them the titbits they enjoy, the wolves and sharp-clawed lions fawned round my men, while they seeing these dread creatures were gripped by fear. They stood there at the gate of the goddess with lovely tresses, and they could hear Circe's sweet voice singing inside, as she went to and fro in front of a vast divine tapestry, weaving the finely-made, lovely, shining work of the goddesses.

These animals were ancestors, heroes and warriors transformed by the magic of the weaving goddess, in the process of being demoted to mortal agent of malefica, bound by her own fateful threads.

If we are to understand the witch then it must be through this archaic image of Potnia Theron, the huntress who poises, winged, often framed by lion or wolf or stag held aloft, one in each hand. She comes down from the sacred mountain. In her warrior form she rides a lion or dragon. She holds serpents. Her breasts stand bare. Her power is drawn from the powers of the natural world and her ability to inspire passion as the force of life. This is the hunger of the she-wolf, explicit sexual desire whose riding out at night will be commemorated in the *Canon Episcopi*, was enfleshed in the Empress Messalina. Witchcraft, wolfcraft as a silver *sestertius* endlessly smelted, secreted in the folds of robes and scudding clouds. This is something which man has sought to deny to woman, with the goddess no longer ruling desire, but increasingly cast as a victim of it. Woman's strength has been made weakness, reaching its apotheosis in the *Malleus Maleficarum* and the demonological literature gone howling backwards through the glass of Revelation. In accepting the demonised figure of the witch whose fall was orchestrated in the classical world, we risk sheathing ourselves in only the outermost skin without first connecting to the power that lies beneath.

It is to the Mistress of Beasts that we must make our supplication, or learn through her cloven messenger, the Devil. Why should we deny the flesh and the hunger behind it which is life itself? It is this which our hide is stretched over. The birch pegs hold taught the invisible form of desire herself resounding. The wolf glyphs initiation into sex and violence, as an inseparable whole. We are tenaciously locked in this struggle and cannot let go.

Virgil, in his 39 BCE *Eclogue*, writes of a sorcerer who took lethal herbs to turn himself into a wolf, the first spoor marks are made, a footprint we can drink from. Perhaps here we have written evidence of the witches' salve:

> *These herbs, these poisons, that were culled in Pontus, it was Mœris*
> *Himself that gave them me. Such herbs are common weeds in Pontus.*
> *Oft by their sorcery I have seen Mœris turn wolf and hide*
> *Within the woods, oft call forth spirits from their deep-dug graves,*
> *And charm away to other fields whole harvests of sown corn.*

This section in *Eclogue* IX must be understood in context. This is part of a woman's love spell which includes incantation, knot magic, poppet magic, burning bay twigs dipped in pitch, and throwing ashes in running water, all carried out by an operator identifying herself with and as Circe. It is a trove of magical techniques. The story of Mœris is inserted as this is clearly love magic empowered by the wolf, who is, by and by, a necromancer. The wolf raises the dead from the jaws of the grave. The wolf's jaws are the grave. As students of Ginzburg's work on the night battles will recognise, the detail of charming away corn in this passage is a clear indication of a continuity of folk practice and the battle for the crops in which the werewolf and witch play an often benefic role.

Mœris as first werewolf is the consort of Mœra, a late name for the goddess of Fate. This is particularly pertinent given the triple thread spell in the passage. Finally the imprecations, in their refrain, *draw from the city, my songs, draw Daphnis home*, yield their result:

See! the embers on the altar have caught with a flickering flame, themselves, of their own accord, while I delay to fetch them. Be it for good! something is there for sure; and Hylax barks in the doorway. May we believe? or do lovers fashion dreams of their own?

The dog is barking at the wolf, here the lover whom she has drawn like the moon back to the hearth, lair and home. It seems strikingly similar to Thracian magic charms still known. Though part of a literary tradition, it is clear that Virgil has culled his scene from folkloric and magical sources which are even at this date, widespread and are not mere day flowers, but draw on deeply archaic roots. There have always been wolves amongst us.

Pliny, in his 73 CE work *Natural History,* doubts the validity of the werewolf, but preserves some of the lore, which doggedly persists amongst the people of the mountains and forests, writing in Book VIII: xxxiv:

> We are bound to pronounce with confidence that the story of men being turned into wolves and restored to themselves again is false – or else we must believe all the tales that the experience of so many centuries has taught us to be fabulous; nevertheless we will indicate the origin of the popular belief, which is so firmly rooted that it classes werewolves among persons under a curse.

He goes on to give a curious example of how such a transformation takes place:

> Evanthes, who holds no contemptible position among the authors of Greece, writes that the Arcadians have a tradition that someone chosen out of the clan of a certain Anthus by casting lots among the family is taken to a certain marsh in that region, and hanging his clothes on an oak-tree swims across the water and goes away into a desolate place and is transformed into a wolf and runs with the others of the same kind for nine years; and that if in that pe-

riod he has refrained from touching a human being, he returns to the same marsh, swims across it and recovers his shape, with nine years' age added to his former appearance; Evanthes also adds the more fabulous detail that he gets back the same clothes.

This seems to be a record of an initiation ordeal, what is missing is the account of the transgression that is ritually enacted. We can surmise that it is, like the example which follows, murder and the ritual eating of human flesh. The oak tree being sacred to Zeus is also perhaps telling. Given the wolf-repelling action of mistletoe we may be looking at a Winter solstice rite. Nine is a sacred number, representing the Ennead and the horizon, but in this context is more likely to glyph the nine months of human gestation. Nine is also given as a critical number in Grimm's *Teutonic Mythology* where the putting on of the wolf-shirt results in a transformation lasting nine days with the return to human form granted on the tenth. Lunar numbers, the kind etched and ochre stained on bone counters by all our ancestors.

Pliny continues to give another critical example of the cause of lycanthropy, tasting human blood, as he tells of the ritual performed on Wolf Mountain in Arcadia:

> Similarly Apollas the author of Olympic Victors relates that at the sacrifice which even at that date the Arcadians used to perform in honour of Lycæan Jove (Zeus Lykaios) with a human victim, Dæmenetus of Parrhasia tasted the vitals of a boy who had been offered as a victim and turned himself into a wolf, and furthermore that he was restored ten years later and trained himself in athletics for boxing and returned a winner from Olympia.

The guilt is somehow expiated in the element of lottery. Only a morsel of entrails spikes the dish which is fallen upon by the ravening adolescent males who are initiated through the nocturnal rite. What became a rite of the wolf king alone began as an initiation for these boys who must become wolves before they can return as men.

Plato used this account, in *The Republic*, where the banquet of Lykaon is an allegory of the tyrant. It remains a persistent accusation levelled at tyrants with ritual cannibalism alleged of African despots, Central American dictators and even the British monarchy. This is not the meaning we seek. It must be remembered that Plato was not an initiate and was deliberately hostile to the symbols of the mysteries, whether cave or wolf.

Here we must examine the ritual act eating of raw flesh and open this with a perceptive quote from Karl Marx, another wolf outside the sheepfold, who wrote in his *Grundrisse*:

> Hunger is hunger, but the hunger that is satisfied with cooked meat eaten with fork and knife is a different kind of hunger from the one that devours raw meat with the aid of hands, nails and teeth.

We must not let our modern selves intervene between us and the smoking entrails. We must look through the haunted eyes of our wolf. Snuff the raw blood, feel our saliva pooling, observe the involuntary swallow. The wolf feast is for the initiates a form of sacred cannibalism, a moment of transformation. Note that the victim in the Lykaios sacrifice is *a boy*, that is kin, just as the candidates for initiation are up until the moment their mouth tastes fateful blood. This is a profound violation, pollution, and this is the critical matter. In eating the boy, they become something forbidden, and this is both an essential moment in their transition to manhood and an act which places them beyond and outside the human realm. When the boys eat of their own blood they literally become wolves and it is clear that there must be a further meaning to this rite than simply a warrior-hood that averts the spiritual danger of killing other men, whose souls will henceforth be linked to them. Again we find ourselves padding back to the dawn of civilisation to scent out our answers and encounter our pre-human past and the origins of witchcraft rather than simply relating tales of the grey fading Wolf Kings of Greece.

If we are to agree with Lévi-Strauss, culture arises only when men eat meat which has been cooked, it is no longer raw (we do not need to have read all four volumes of his *Mythologiques* but can gnaw straight on the sweetmeats). They have returned from the hunt to the cooking fires, not selfishly devoured it apart from the women. Therefore the eating of raw meat is revolutionary, though not in the sense of Marx, rather as a transgression it overturns the existence of all human culture. By sharing the kill, the adolescents are partaking of the same blood. They are affirming the kinship of the bund. They have become the mouth of the mother but like her are beyond human society, and this is where she is encountered. The blood that they are weaned on is not simply the blood of the animal, it is in a real sense their own blood as they suckle on the entrails of the gaping carcass. The mouths plunging in the trough of the slit belly is an unmistakably maternal and menstrual image. Here we see how blood and milk are cognate. In hermetic terms this is given the image of the pelican; in witchcraft terms, mother wolf as Mistress of the Beasts, it is La Papessa in the Tarot. Note here the pun on the word *pap* for breast. Furthermore, it is the dove, as full moon, whose breast alone amongst birds seeps milk. And it is this dove which crowns the Minoan Mistress. This is the power that women must retake, our generation must suckle more wolves.

The wolves' feast is different from that of the hunters who would kill (or scavenge) and return with the butchered meat to the cooking fires and hearth of the women. To eat of the uncooked meat and be tainted by the blood would be forbidden. It is the women who remove the taboo from the meat by cooking the blood out of it, just as they are *cooked* in that they are no longer menstruating. This is where the mystery is truly revealed. Hunting is not a male mystery in isolation. In 'primitive' societies the link between menstruation and the blood of the animals killed in the hunt is explicit. The blood of the women and the blood of the animals is seen as identical, the hunter's spear is the phallus, hunting is sex.

Meat is therefore identified with sex. Those who try to break the bond between sex and the hunt, of which war is one parabola, do themselves an injustice. Love and war are Janus faced, as they are in essence the same blood, the drive which is *eros*, the creation and life and motive power of the universe which is also *thanatos*. In a very real sense the grail, the cup of abominations, is the mixed blood of all living things, and Babalon the Mistress of the Beasts with whom we honour and share the kill.

It is this complex of menstrual taboos which sent the hunters ranging after their prey. The sign of menstrual blood at the dark moon triggered the organisation of the hunt. The fire was extinguished, or tended by girls and women entered into deliberate seclusion. Arguably this is when witchcraft was practised, as a female mystery in the absence of men, that is by definition all males old enough to be blooded in the hunt. Menstrual blood rituals are incestuous in the sense that at this time women are secluded from their marriage partners but not their kin. This is the time to prepare the salve.

Solar eclipse equals sudden menstruation, and therefore the putting out of cooking fires and a clamour of pans, this is a new moon phenomena. Lunar eclipse is a further disaster, in that it makes the moon bloody at full. Both these events have profound witchcraft implications. The dark moon requires menstruation and therefore the spilling of blood: of woman, animal and man. Therefore blood is the offering at the dark moon, and dew is the response at the full moon as the souls of the slain return. In this way we find the sacraments of witchcraft laid before us, and the necessary preparations of the dark moon that ready us for attending the sabbat feast.

Though a contested idea in our species, lunar menstrual synchrony may have been the norm for our ancestors, with bloody raw dark moon and sexual congress at the full magnetically aligning us to a tidal hunting pattern. As this is not a specialist text, these ideas are perforce charcoal lines, and readers are directed to the study of the anthropological literature, in particular aspects of the ground-breaking thesis of Chris Knight which builds upon the intuitions of Shuttle and Redgrove. What I am describing is an ideal abstract, a

124

myth which is within my remit as a storyteller. The man or woman who becomes a wolf is engaged in a cyclical transformation that takes them outside of culture. For women this is a given, they are periodic, but for men this requires ritual action. The witchcraft of men is thus built and dependent upon the blood of women. Blood must also flow for men to be initiated. Whipping, subincision, circumcision, scarification and tattooing are among the ritual actions that can be performed. This does not imply simple masochism.

What we see in the wolf feast is a deliberate transgression of the blood eating rule, and this invokes a curse. The men become wolves, just as was within the power of Circe, and just like the boys they have been 'tricked' into it. This tricking or metis is the magic of shamanic culture and is a lupine quality. Eating the bloody kill is the same as the gluttony and its implied sexual incontinence which afflicts the crew of the Argo. They do not however become their ancestors, who are the ancestors of all hunters; the wolves, lions, and bears. In a punishment for their lack of self-mastery they are transformed into swine. But we must keep in mind that Homer is late to the feast and has the agenda of his Age. Circe as vestige of the Great Goddess and Mistress of the Beasts is being derided as much as the actions of the men, who are transformed after their own image just as Apulieus becomes an ass rather than an owl in his later misadventure. Note that the wolf transformation is often called a curse, exactly the same word patriarchy ascribes to menstruation.

But what if, rather than seeing the eating of raw meat as usurping female power, a motif found in all aboriginal societies, it is performed under the auspices of the Mistress of the Beasts? How complicit are the men and boys in this ritual trickery? Surely there is also a fear being evoked here of that most dangerous and magical of substances, raw menstrual blood, and its incommensurable power. It is the ultimate magical salve.

The use of the boy in the Lykaios sacrifice is still commensurate with these ideas, as the boy who is not a man is still literally part of the blood of his mother. What if we can taste the forbidden blood and be dedicated to the Mistress? What if we become wolves in her service? I suggest that witchcraft represents such an inversion, a reversion of the patterns of abuse and domination that have enslaved women and divided the sexes in setting men upon women as untrammelled appetites. We do not need wolf kings, we need wolf packs who understand that their first allegiance is to the mountain mother.

We circle back, howling round. Calls seem everywhere now. The wolf will surely show itself to us as more than shadow. The blood feast of the boy makes him a man, but in the unstable eruption of adolescence, the insatiable hunger, the sexual incontinence, he must be exiled as a wolf before he can be welcomed once more at the hearth. His relationship to women must change. He needs to be socialised within the pack. We however range more widely, having a further need, that of the Shaman, whose night flights pre-figure the success of the hunt.

Let us begin then to construct our rites on these principles. Other than the tasting of blood, how does this transformation occur?

The 1 CE *Satyricon* of Gaius Petronicus tells of a man becoming a wolf by stripping naked and urinating in a circle around his clothes before running into the woods. This is done because male urine contains testosterone and marks territory in exactly the same way wolves do. The nudity is the stripping away of the socialised self. The man become wolf is therefore excluded from the circle of humankind. The setting for this scene is a graveyard at midnight under a full moon. The werewolf who absconds is wounded and the wound found upon the man the next day, a common motif in the myths. Is this a vestige of the bloody initiation of tribal rites?

In Portuguese and Galician lore, the werewolf also strips naked to affect the transformation yet in Northern Europe nudity is not always a practical option. We have already mentioned the alternative method of donning a charmed skin, belt or girdle.

Other accounts have men rolling in the dirt to become the animal which last did so. We see this behaviour with dogs when they roll in fox urine. Perhaps this lore is imitative of that behaviour. Smell is our most forgotten and archaic sense, one which we respond to on a purely instinctual level. Though magic uses incense in ritual, the importance of perfume is often forgotten. This is why those working with animal transformation often find that they eschew all chemical products and counterfeit scents. Doing this work will also change your diet. Processed cooked foods, refined sugars and fats will quickly become distasteful, they do not smell right. The odour of man needs to be sweated out of us and our natural smell return, something our culture prefers to mask with anodyne florals and 'clean' notes of sandalwood and cedar that are as artificial as the labs which clone them. Sex is about scent, and will return, as will all the senses when we encounter our animal again. This is an experience reported by both hunters and soldiers in the field who relate a sharpening of eyesight, smell, touch, hearing and that elusive prickling of the sixth sense. Learn to trust this again.

What we can further surmise is that the wolf transformation was at times aided by the use of magical plants. The pharmacopeia runs from henbane to amanita muscaria to belladonna, and the effects from soporific to stimulant. But the drugs required for war are not necessarily those of the night flights. A salve which extends waking is surely no use in sending out the shift? Perhaps we can prise open the jaws of this contradiction by examining the imagery of the 2 CE Kobyakovo torque and the problems in its interpretation. The gold and turquoise relief shows lycanthropic belted warriors battling a dragon whilst in the centre of the piece is an older bearded man, sat cross-legged on a mat, holding a bowl and with sword across his lap. This much is undisputed. Yulia Ustinova, in her paper on the relic, claims his eyes are closed to bolster her supposition of trance, though even a cursory examination of the image shows that this is not the case: his eyes are wide open. She further compares his posture to the shaman on the Gundestrup cauldron, though that figure is pressing heel to perineum and not strictly cross-legged. It is unsteady evidence at best. This curious artefact is then suggested as showing two levels of initiation, that of the warrior as wolf who goes out dressed in skins, and that of the band leader who in meditation leaves his body to fight supernatural enemies. What cannot be known is the contents of the bowl which he has supped on. One particular candidate is ephedra, a warrior drug if ever there was one. Perhaps this moon plant, this haoma, was the milk they suckled on. The related amphetamines are still military issue and were the fuel of the wolf-totemed Wehrmacht. But even here we cannot be sure that he is not the master of the medicine who has mixed and dispensed it. We cannot see if his lips or beard are wet, but his open eyes strongly suggest that he has. He is engaged in the act of seeing. A soporific which initially seemed the better choice for night flight and introversion of the band leader, and the stimulant for the physical war and extroversion of the adolescents, once examined becomes treacherous.

We have demonstrably lost the sense of sacred around the stimulants, and the god-like nature they bestow, taking on Eastern ideas of introversion as trance and missing the sacristy of extroversion and action. War is as sacred as the hunt. Often *amanita muscaria* is given as a suggestion for the disputed Haoma, rather than ephedra, perhaps because of this bias. For Ginzburg it is because of his (unproven) Siberian origin myth. On top of this we have layered our cherished ideas of witchcraft and the salve of the demonologists whom we will encounter next. It seems that there is no universal wolf medicine beyond blood, and no quick fix or substitute for a fully functioning and supported endocrine system. This is where research should be placed, or we are at risk of discarding our bodies like cartridge cases. Wolf work requires herbal adrenal support, it also requires guising and dance, if not blooding in battle itself.

The demonologists faced the same dilemma with the werewolf as they did with the sabbat, and grappled with whether the transformation was physical, or a form of illusion. Jean Bodin in his 1580 *Demonomanie* believes it to be a physical transformation yet this is at odds with the orthodox teaching on the matter established by Augustine in his *City of God* who comments on the story of Circe:

I say that you must not believe that any man can be transformed into a wolf or pig, that this is merely a ghost, or an appearance deceiving the eyes, or created in the imagination.

In the same passage, Augustine affirms that the devil can make people fly and claims that witches have no power, the devil simply responds to their empty ritual actions, it is not the acts or the individuals who possess any force. It is a poor argument that is designed to strip the power from the increasingly wretched figure of the witch.

In his 1612 *On the Inconstancy of Witches*, De Lancre takes Augustine to account, suggesting that previously the acts of sorcerors were less well known due to their scarce numbers which were now reaching epidemic levels in his fevered pronouncements. Whilst allowing the possibility of dream flight, he staunchly insisted on the primacy of their physical reality.

To the contrary, James I, in his 1597 *Dæmonologie,* blames lycanthropy on *a superabundance of melancholy*. It is an affliction of Saturn, which at the very least references the eating of children. He does not credit a physical transformation but dutifully cites the seven years Nebuchadnezzar spent as an Ox (Daniel 4:33) as does Cornelius Agrippa. Given the paucity of wolves in scripture, this is the most cited verse. Francisco Maria Guazzo in his 1628 *Compendium Maleficarum* also sees it as an illusion that *witches turn men into beasts*, he blames *ointments and charms* for the transformation and gives this ability to witches empowered by the devil. Circe has evidently not been dispelled, but has been joined by the folk fiend who is now taking a leading role.

As we have found in the approach to the sabbat, the demonologists are riven over the nature of animal transformation and how to separate it from the 'authentic' miracles of the gospel. The salve is often conveniently used to distinguish between the pious ecastasy of the prophets and the impious actions of the devil-inspired witches. What is clearly not scant is folk belief that the wolf is not all that it seems, in a list of suspects that notably includes toad, cat and hare. This is not simply an elite dialogue.

The wolf as natural enemy of the lamb was bound to suffer in an increasingly zealous age. Alongside the warrior wolf is an established European magical shape-shifting complex that at times overlaps and then almost entirely replaces it. Ginzburg relates how self-confessed werewolves fought with devils and witches to prevent the loss of the crops in great night battles over the fertility of the land. But even the account Ginzburg provides of the old werewolf Thiess contains the detail that his nose was broken by a sorcerer during one such battle. In the realm of night flight, there are physical consequences, and lines which may seem clear, between waking, sleeping, dream and physical attendance, do not correspond with our cherished reason.

The trial testimony Ginzburg cites was contrary to the growing demonisation of the werewolf in the 15th century. He argues that the werewolf and his kin are part of the deeper strata of shamanism, stating: 'In both cases the animal metamorphoses and the cavalcades astride animals symbolically express ecstsasy: the temporary death indicated by the egress of the soul from the body in animal form.'

This seems a little too tidy and psychologised. For Ginzburg these armies of the dead and incongruous testimony were increasingly forced to conform into the demonological form of the sabbat by the inquisitors. For him the female-led night flights or wild hunts become the devil-led sabbat. There is a great cache of this material, from Sicilian *donas de fuera*, Hungarian *táltos* to Corsican *mazzeri* to explore. They engage in individual actions and massed ritual battles. The army of the dead ranges across Europe, led by different figures from Odin to Diana but most often the Good Mistress. The Mighty Dead are often fierce dogs or wolves. It would be remiss to ignore the actual existence of night revels, not as out of body experience, but as physical actions. So we find physical processions of animal-guised adolescent youths passing from house to house and receiving food and drink. It is a grand unruly Lupercalia celebrated at the beginning and end of the ritual year, a stormy, rutting *vouarouverie* which leers wolfishly out of the night. But this does not explain the sabbat; it is a grey river of bodies that feeds into it.

130

Such a Lupercalia is an annual or bi-annual event. At Easter, the wolf takes the lamb, in dead of Winter, the stag is downed. These are physical ritual events for the whole community, times of misrule and animalistic sex. It is a social reconciliation with the ancestors, and a warning, just as the sabbat is. This hurly-burly is one face of witch-craft. Even in seemingly open events there are private ritual moments not divulged to outsiders or those beyond the core ritual group. A living witchcraft needs to re-establish or introduce these events to give meaning back to their community.

But the wolves do not stop running. There is a hunger which can-not be sated. The wolf transgresses the boundary of the village but lives in the wild among its own kind. The witch is a ritual specialist whose animal transformation is triggered by the moon, and there are thirteen such moments every year. Witchcraft is outside the village, now sprawled into city, apart from it by necessity, but still acting in relation to it. We mediate between the demands of these worlds and as the balance shifts, so too must we. Our survival depends upon it.

Ginzburg sees the vital human myth as going into the beyond and returning, neglecting to state that this is something only the heroic dead can do, and demonstrate as much in the cyclical Wild Hunt. He does not explain every aspect of the sabbat. What differs between hunt and sabbat is that the hunt moves through social space, the sabbat is a communion celebrated outside of it. The wild hunt can be seen, as it is an incursion of the dead into the world of the living. The sabbat in clear distinction must be participated in, we must fly to it, it does not pass by our door. The hunt is a roaming feast whilst the sabbat is an appointed place, on the mountain of the Mistress. The sabbat in a sense stands still, it is outside of time, neither going nor returning but coinciding. At core is a sense of being present in the moment, a paradoxical union of life and death which can only be reached through participating bodily in the dance.

The noise and clamour of the wild hunt marks it out as akin to a dark moon event but it is not simply that, it is a profoundly chthonic one where mother earth herself disgorges the menstruum of the dead, just as Inanna returns from the realm of Ereshkigal with her retinue of *gallas*. Folklore accounts vary but the element which characterises the wild hunt is the kind of storm that arises in Autumn and Winter in dark Europe and in particular the days between Yule and Twelfth Night, not the state of the moon which is essentially obscured by clouds. Those who participate in the hunt are both black and blackened, a cavalcade of mythical heroes, hounds and ghosts. This is not the full moon of the sabbat, but the bloody moon of extinguished fires and noise, of a Sun grown weak and finally driven to bay. Rather than the inversion of the sabbat, in the hunt the elements are explicitly mixed, sky and earth sundered by earthquake, thunder and lightning, not whipped and spinning about a point but broken on the anvils of a storm passing over the land. It may be important to note here that the mushroom is considered the child of the lightning and flecked like a deer.

Such a hunt and battle is not the sole preoccupation of the human wolf. But as wolves we need to pour through the streets as the dead, as ancestry, as vengeance. We are the generation which is caught in the storm and ours is a bloody ritual that must be performed. Our fealty is sworn to sacred blood.

We can now divine the whole chain of meaning which creates witchcraft. This is the essence of the mythic structure, neither a definitive nor an exhaustive series of events, but a necessary panorama to take in.

Man learns to hunt following the example of the wolf. The hunt is guided by the visions and dreams of the shaman who has negotiated the deaths of the animals with the Mistress of the Beasts. Men enact the drama of the hunt dressed as animals; this is the basis of all ritual. Menstruation controls the timing of these ritual events. The feast is celebrated communally at the full moon. This is the sabbat where sex and food are shared. Boys are initiated into this cycle with blood and spend a period beyond the bounds of society. Girls are initiated into womanhood with menstruation and cyclical exclusion within society. Woman, witch, shaman and hunter all have status and roles.

The city state arises out of agriculture and breeds war. Men as wolves are initiated into killing other men. The hunt extends into war. The wolf becomes increasingly ambivalent with the domestication of herd animals and the growing of cereal crops; though it is still roped into fertility rites, the focus is becoming martial. The contract with nature has been broken, provoking a sense of guilt. The shaman is replaced by the king and a politicised priesthood. Women's magic driven to the periphery. The Great Goddess is becoming the witch.

Christian monotheism places a monopoly on spiritual agency. The wolf is now a pagan pariah. Ecstasy is not an applicable spiritual technology. The ritual hunt is reserved for the king. The Mistress of Beasts is replaced by the devil as wild nature and the force of sex: horned Venus, garbed as Saturn. The commons are enclosed. The wolf is now enemy. The full moon celebration is painted as an orgiastic child killing cult. The night ride whether the goddess is Diana, Herodias or Holda is now a flight on animals to the sabbat. Hunt and feast have become aggregated into one awful carnival whose meaning is effaced. The witch and sorcerer are anti-social terrorists plotting to destroy Christendom.

Should we stop here and chase our tails? We have not yet run our quarry to ground. We must go on. The wolf is the shadow of man. We have hunted the same prey. But we have fallen out with these brothers and sisters, to our detriment and their extinction. Let us decide to play the game again. Let us turn over the cards of Dame Fortune. Trump XVIII The Moon reveals even dogs are transformed on certain nights into their ancestors, and that it is blood which provides the key. Through this slim fence slip once more the gaunt wolves into the city, our throats erupting into song.

VIII

Flayed by sun rays
She is first
Among martyrs
Nations fear her
Blood heavy promise
A star
Pricked into
Adventure's hand
Inanna guides us
Burn clean cedar
Cities with hymns
Honey smeared
Terminals crackle
At her set table
Angels attend
From morning
To sunrise
Phalanxes pass

Fifteen

The cup of poison shall thy lovers see.

We stand naked beneath the full moon, silvered as the cedars. Our feet are bare on the earth, our heads are consumed with the heights. Having responded to the summons of the devil, the owl eyed, bear handed, deer rumped master. Having dreamt, having flown, we are prepared for the Queen of the Sabbat by stripping down to our skins. We are egalitarian in our shedding of artifice. We are as the serpent who, like the pocked bone ovum of the heavens, is cyclically consumed and renewed. Beneath the glamour of moonlight a transformation occurs.

It takes guts to stand naked and unashamed before your lover, your mirror, your moonlight. To silence the small voices, the imperfections that mark us, however statuesque, as not unchanging, but as submerged in the river of endless time. We are worn not smooth in such a river but lined, stretched, scarred, contorted, veined as the landscape itself. So too is our witchcraft. We ache with time whose blood clock has measured our tread to and from the sabbat mount. Our backs become bent around sticks, stangs and brooms which we no longer hold, but now hold us. Flesh sags reticent, hair comes away in our hands, teeth loosen in wasted gums. An effort of breath wheezes out of our puncturing lungs. Age lowers heads that can no longer support the weight of horns. The old wolf lags back too, knowing he cannot run even this last deer to ground. The pace slows to a hobble, to resignation, to death. The hunt has cost us dearly. Yet our frailty is riven with such strength. Even time can cease, for however many heartbeats, on one sacred night. As our bodies fail, the moon draws us on. It lifts us as it will lift our hollow bones when the marrow no longer inundates us with blood. We recognise that this is sacrifice, that this is the culmination of ordeal. It is not for us to apologise, it is only for us to make our tread, however burdened, a dance. We are animated by the moonlight, by the midnight sun in his secret cavern. The rules of the day run widdershins.

This is where the circling begins. The linking of hands that affirms we are not isolate, but coven. The linking of hands that makes us one flesh and one family. The linking of hands that stretches back through ancestry. The linking of hands that binds us in secrecy and mystery. It is this simple, and this profound. Within this circle, the great rite unfolds.

The goddess is not the moon, this, a misunderstanding. She is Time herself.

It is time which the same moon marks through all its phases, from the dark moon of menstrual blood to her potency at full. These aspects can be experienced as separate and distinct goddesses and rites, yet it is the sabbat which marks the moment of immanence in the cycle of flux and flow. The full moon reveals the true queen of the sabbat whose face is no longer veiled in shadow.

In keeping with tradition, the goddess is never named, but is referred to in oblique terms. Red, Black or White Goddess simply describes her aspect. Other names are ciphers, blinds, riddles, points of origin. One of the most enduring of these is as the Goddess Fifteen, and perhaps number is the way in which we can most clearly begin to envisage her, rather than in the competing cultural forms. She is essential, that which endures across the gulf of time. The moon, like the witch herself is simply a mask. It is as the Goddess Fifteen that these vectors converge on the sabbat ground. This is the underlying unity witchcraft reveals.

We do not need a complex method of gematria to unlock the

meaning of this number. The notched eagle bones of the Upper Palæolithic have had this arithmetic tooled into them. Incised on batons, or wands, the lunar count was reckoned. It has been calibrated with precision, from fingers to pebbles sown in pits, to bone slates, and hung pendant on our necks to lie between our breasts. These bone wands had a ritual function, about which we can only speculate. If they were used against the drum, we have lost the beat until we learn to listen to our hearts again. From our furthest ancestors we have only images and not story, the sorcerer, the herds, the red rubbed vulvic glyphs, the pendulant breasts of stalactites, the silent goddess with neither feet nor mouth but insistently scored pubic triangle. Yet though we cannot reconstruct with any certainty, we are not so different from these ancestors in physiology; perhaps our witchcraft has similar concerns, the core of our ritual actions seeking to delineate or unfold the same mysteries of life and death. Before writing, this notation spidered its way across our mental terrain, intense with detail. It would be impossible for this not to have a menstrual meaning, perhaps in the symbolic form we have already discussed and which reaches its apotheosis in the sabbat.

It is from the dreams and memories flowing from these bones that John of Patmos enfleshed his monstrous theogony, and which encoded the mystery of Woman and thus fledged the latter witch cult. It is these bones which are our reliquaries, whether still set in their barrows or jostling in ossuaries. Bones speak.

The lunar calendar predates agriculture and civilisation. This reveals man, as Alexander Marschack puts it, both *time factored* and *time factoring*, not simply a tool maker. We can remove the lazy habit of gender which creeps into our speech, and say that it is more likely that this symbolic language was created and preserved by women, that they possessed these ritual tools themselves. Witchcraft throbs with a lunar menstrual rhythm. When we look at the acts and tools of the craft: the doll, thread, knot, needle, loom, wheel, poison, plant, chant, hearth, fire, home, it is an inevitable conclusion that these are female mysteries and have been since the dawn of time. But the hunt and the rites of men are also presided over by this pre-eminent figure as Mistress of the Beasts, whom the sorcerer, or devil, is beneath, and these separate streams flow together in the sexual conjoining of the full moon sabbat.

On the wall of the cave of Laussel we see the goddess holding a horn, into it are incised thirteen parallel lines marking out the lunar year. Robert Graves also gives the sacred number of his imagined White Goddess as 13, and then continues: 'in so far as her courses coincide with the Solar Year, but 15 in so far as the full moon falls on the 15th day of each lunation.' The figure on the wall of Laussel is, as we must note, ochred red.

Can we find a continuity of this knowledge? Again Marschack can be cited, in his dogged resistance to the idea that events in pre-history were a succession of *suddenly* moments. He divined that this hid our own lack of comprehension, and our inability to read the evidence correctly. This 'suddenly' has led others into wild speculation on alien intervention, orbiting death stars, lost civilisations and genetic splicing, and these have proved even poorer explanations to vault us into comprehension of our modern plight than the passing over of the sciences. Archaeology has hidden behind such words as *magic* and *ritual* to mean incomprehensible, gibberish and therefore to be ignored by homo scientist. The same is true of *witchcraft*, or *voodoo* and their misuse in common parlance. The thread stretches thinly from the cave, its triple weave still tight and true, but the difficulty is the form in which the evidence takes, in that it asks us to draw the story from it. Sometimes it seems we must divine the labyrinth from tattered thread alone. But the evidence is there, in musical tones, the arched harp, the flute, the symbolic language of art, gesture on fresco and vase, the repetition of phrase embedded in an oral transmission, burnt seeds and the arrangement of the dead. Witchcraft does not arise *ex nihilo*.

Are these scant indications, or a treasury? The answer depends upon our techne, the mental tools we bring to bear, the forms we find within our bodies. This work can only ultimately be done through poetry, and its living expression as ritual. It is a memento mori, a lych gate through which only the hero and witch can tread. It is the answer to a post-modern morass of emptiness where signified and signifier are an arbitrary arrangement in which meaning is ultimately absent. The mythic inoculates us from such despair.

Lascaux is closed, corrupting with breath and botched conservation attempts. Green mould will devour the last surging horses and bellowing stags left to us. I am not a palaeontologist, so the cave that I have made my pilgrimage to in this journey has been John's. I have not reached an impenetrable back wall, but have descended into his cowled skull and the dreams whose skein has taken me into a primordial past and the unchanging laws of the Underworld to bring this story back.

My understanding is that witchcraft is not a continuous cult, but demonstrably part of an historical process rather than simply an aberration that coagulated out of the minds of the Inquisition. Now that the bones of Murray's and Graves' theses have been picked clean we can in this generation examine the notches graven upon them and discover a poetic and hitherto unexplained language; one which our detractors will no doubt despise as a jumble of rude marks and coincidence. Yet above all these hangs the moon as our proof, between our legs runs honey and blood. She teaches us in dreams.

For the lunar calendar to exist required it to have embodied meaning, one which meshed into a series of species and events, of salmon runs and rutting deer and moulting bison and sleeping and waking bears. It is a cycle of seasons over which a Mistress of the Beasts prevailed. For us to engage with the mythic, we must be attuned to its many pulses over which the moon rules. But crisis intervenes.

The Eden of an ice-glazed Europe opening into spring and countless herds was cut short by man. The late Pleistocene saw overkill, a perfection of hunting techniques which brought about the extinction of the mega fauna by hunters. This theory is supported by the slaughter enacted by humans as they spread into the Americas, and the inability of species to adapt and respond to the actions of this new and hitherto unknown predator. It does not sit well with ideas of shamanic culture as attuned to its environment and enacting a killing balance. Clayton Eshleman in his *Juniper Fuse* is mindful of this, and sees even the cave art as a record of the fall of man, our loss of animality, and the very animals themselves, recreated deep in the living rock of our literal underworld as we seek recourse in dreams for our severed state. I would place this fall later, when the plough knifed into the alluvial soil. The guilt for this action has not been expiated. It troubles us for a reason.

If these lunar ideas were cultural currency, then we would expect to find a vestige of them in the fertile crescent of Mesopotamia, in Egypt, and the birth of civilisation. Could there be a shaft, a moonbeam, illuminating from the Upper Paleolithic into the Mesolithic into the Neolithic and beyond? The move to the city, and our loss of a way of life was bound to engender a mythical shift. I place witchcraft within this furrow, this opening wound, attempting to knit and reconcile a balance perhaps forever lost. Yet the moon, though changing, remained the same. Now it was not simply the salmon run, the story of the first flowers in the meadow, but the song of the grain. There was no jagged break, but a million tributary rivers carrying us on. Her sex runs wet.

Gerald Massey wrote: 'It was as mother-moon that Ishtar of Akkad was designated "Goddess 15" — she being named from the full moon in a month of 30 days.' And so our goddess slips from the reed banks and finds herself within a second cave at the temple heights, above the inundation of the flood. Massey's work is a mound of broken pottery, a mass of fascinating shards, but not a stable foundation or sound methodology. We must excavate here with care. Ishtar is of course primarily associated with Venus, but he is accurate in giving the fifteenth day for the full moon; both Venus and the Moon are symbolic of fire and flood. The role of Venus is the sacred marriage of the sun and moon in the five days that mesh their cycle. This is the pentagram of witchcraft. It was the fifteenth when she descended to the underworld and Ereshkigal, and here her character is revealed as overturning order. We still have one unanswered question: how can she, as Venus on the day of the full moon, descend into the labyrinth of the bloody dark moon? The resolution of this paradox is given in Mystery.

Ishtar it must be remembered is not one goddess, but the name of many. Every city has a goddess in her name. The Ishtar of Nineveh is commemorated in the prayer of the Assyrian King Assurnasirpal, a text with clearly archaic elements. In the prayer he twice refers to setting up 14 goddesses:

And thou oh Ishtar did make great my name,
And thou hast given to the faithful salvation and reward,
It went forth from thy mouth to renew the burned gods,
The falling temples I renewed,
The overthrown gods I built up, I restored to their places,
The fourteen goddesses were exalted, I established them forever.

Could it be that these are lunar aspects, with Ishtar herself as the Goddess 15? This is a conclusion that other scholars have also reached, as the reference to the 14 is followed by the creation of a lavish bed for the statue of Ishtar to recline upon. The Assyrian records also make clear that Ishtar begins to be identified as Bilit, a name which began as an epithet and survives in the thirteenth spirit of the Ars Goetia as Bileth.

Ishtar is offered wine, Assurnasirpal describing it as *the joy of thy heart*. It is also used in the central rite of kingship, the lion hunt:

Over the lions which I killed, I lifted up the bow, the might of Ishtar Queen of Battle, I offered over them a prayer, I poured wine over them.

The bow is always a lunar symbol, and thus an attribute of this goddess who appears in forms both naked and fully armed. The lion is both her mount, and sacrifice to her. As woman she is the motive power of life, expressed in the erotic frenzy of Love and War. Witch-craft presides over these upheavals.

As we have previously mentioned, it is in the Babylonian creation epic, *Enuma Elish,* that we find *šabattu* as the fifteenth day. In the story, Marduk creates the world by dividing the waters of Tiamat in what is clearly the prototype of the biblical Genesis. The binding and treading are also themes in the Greek Titanomachy and thence the treatment of Satan in Revelation. This act of division was ritually en-acted each Vernal equinox with the release of a dove whose parabolic flight was cut in half with a sword. It is a profoundly shocking image, one which encompasses menstruation, sex, the overthrow of the god-dess, the half-moon and the division of day and night, salt and fresh waters, above and below.

Ishtar is also this dove, the daughter. John Allegro gives her name as deriving from *uštar,* the womb. This is a safer etymology than the later fairy rings he becomes lost in. She has inherited the charac-teristics of her great grandmother. She is defined by her youth and vigour. She has this terrible connection because she has been to the underworld, the inverted city, the labyrinth and, ultimately, cave. She transcends categories of chthonic and ouranic, violates them, returns to earth with her retinue of demons.

Aphrodite is but one of the love goddesses who inherited this dove. The dove is the woman, and as the symbol of love represents not the phallus, as falsely given in Christian symbolism, but the womb, the goddess. The dove is female, her breast weeps milk; to use it as a symbol of the holy ghost or as a spermognostic emblem is a grave error. There is another inversion to insert here, in the Babylo-nian flood myth it is not the dove who finds land but the crow.

In an agriculture based on irrigation, rain and flood were criti-cal. Trickling moisture which woke the spring flowers, which had presaged the movement of the herds was joined with a growing awareness of storm. The great threat to the grain was drought and inundation. Too wet, too hot are the eternal threats of woman, neither cooked nor raw, but mutable and lunar, a rhythm punctuated by capricious devastation, whom Inanna likewise embodied, which magic sought to propitiate and harness.

If we are searching for an origin of the goddess of witchcraft, then we must consider Inanna-Ishtar as the primal spring. In *The Red Goddess* I was able to trace the history of the goddess of Revelation back to this source. This is a bold thesis, so let us be sure of our evidence. In *Persian Literature: Ancient and Modern*, Elizabeth A. Reed examines the sixth tablet of the Gilgamesh epic, the oldest known version of the tale, and is shocked at the depiction of Ishtar of Uruk:

> She here appears as the queen of witchcraft, resembling the Hecate of the Greeks in her funereal abode. Indeed, Hecate was babbled to be the daughter of Asteria, which is merely the Greek form of the name Ishtar, and Pausanius mentions an Astrateia whose worship was brought to Greece from the East.

As we can see, this is a native Greek hypothesis, not a lapis overlay in order to complete the mosaic. The implications of this are profound; it is Inanna-Ishtar who underlies our entire conception of the witch and whose image resurges in the incubation of John. She goes further still:

> The character of Ishtar as presented in this tablet is apparently a prototype not only of Hecate, but also of Medea, whose chariot was drawn by winged serpents, and the cauldron or pot, which Ishtar filled with her magic herbs, suggests the statement of Ovid that Medea on one occasion spent no less than nine days and nights in collecting herbs for her cauldron. [*Metamorphoses*, VII, 234] The character of Ishtar may have also suggested that of Circe, who 'mixed the potion, fraudulent of soul, The poison mantled in a golden bowl,' and she loved Ulysses and Ishtar loved Izdubar, even though she had transformed all of his companions into swine.

Ishtar is indeed berated in the tablet itself by Gilgamesh/Izdubar who says: *the cup of poison shall thy lovers see*. This poison chalice is for us a grail, one which is present throughout the biblical literature until the Harlot of Revelation proffers it to our lips. It is the cup that transverses the coven circle. Inanna-Ishtar, our lady of lions, is the Mistress of the Beasts. Ishtar too is the mother of harlots, and it was the temple hierodule who knew the secrets of sex, of contraception, who if she became pregnant was put to death by burning; the same fate that awaits the medieval witch.

If that was not enough, we have the final piece. In column II of the tablet under consideration, we find the story of the king whom Ishtar changed into a leopard: 'and his own dogs bit him to pieces. No one can doubt here that we see the original of the Greek fable of Actæon, the hero who offended the goddess Diana, when she revenged herself by changing him into a deer.'

Though Reed's work is at times dated, Fontenrose, in his study *Python*, sums much of this up, with Ishtar's aspects helping illuminate the focus of his own work on the Delphic myth:

> In contemplating Ishtar it becomes easy to understand the iden-
> tification of Artemis with Hekate, of a goddess of fertility and
> the hunt with a goddess of ghosts and witchcraft. In the myth of
> the descent to the lower world Ishtar came back to earth amidst a
> rout of ghosts and demons. Just so did Hekate lead her bands of
> spirits and bogeys at night; and Artemis' band of huntress nymphs
> that bring death to intruders are the corresponding midday troop,
> associated with the wild panic of siesta time. Both Hekate and
> Artemis lead the wild hunt.

The debt that the Greeks owe to the East has been further explored in modern scholarship by M.L. West's phenomenal *The East Face of Helicon*, and David Reid West's *Some Cults of Greek Goddesses & Female Daimons of Oriental Origin* which settles conclusively that Hekate is not of Thracian origin. Inanna, Ishtar, Medea, Circe, Hekate, Diana,

Artemis, such is the progression of the witch, joined in her journey by the queens of the fairy mounds, by local legends and a seething body of clerical lies.

Put simply, there is no 'suddenly' in this history of the witch. She has flowed from the fertile crescent, both East and West, following the lines of lattitude, and only later found her horned consort in the North, one of many lovers. She has stood upon the temples and towers of the East beneath a gibbous moon. She has trodden the Indus valley and coupled with Shiva. Her stellar appellations all in essence mean radiant light, the symbol of divinity. This is our lineage, which some prefer to know as blood.

As we have seen, Inanna-Ishtar has bestowed her DNA upon a wide profusion of goddesses, and like them undergone a process of demonisation; no example is more revealing than that of Lilith, who as a very minor mythological figure has been a convenient caricature of the far greater power standing behind her. In this shift the child-killing aspect is emphasised and a confusion between this night-flying demoness and our lady deliberately cultivated to fit the demands of patriarchy. Attempts to read Lilith's mythography through the Jewish myths and then wrangle them into a witchcraft cosmology may be well meaning, but do not have the benefit of actually approaching the Sumerian sources. The beginning of history is passed over in a flight to late medieval Jewish mysticism. Lilith is the incubus who is transfected into medieval semen-stealing nightmares. Is our witchcraft purely this malign? Or are we mistakenly nurturing their lies in our cradle?

Inanna-Ishtar, the great goddess, is hidden by racial prejudice, slur and propaganda. She is effaced by a classical scholarship that favours a cleaned-up Greece and Rome to a Venus Vulgaris, a Queen of Harlots, for our cultural origins. Modern paganism has simply trailed in this wake and drawn us the picture of a witch from her marginalised and disgraced place in later literature. It is essential that we understand that history begins in Sumer.

A clear example of this over-writing is the Queen of Night relief,

one of the treasures of the ancient world. In it, a goddess stands
on the back of two lions which she holds in clawed bird feet, she
is flanked by owls, winged and wears a horned crown. This is an
object for veneration as the figure is naked and gazes directly out.
We can tell it is a goddess from the horned crown and the ring and
rod devices lofted in her hands, these are reserved for divinity. Flecks
show that her skin was as red as any dakini, the wings feathered in
black, white and red, the background not lapis but black as night.
The identity of the figure has been much disputed, it is a stripped
antiquity, and so its place of origin remains unknown. Originally it
was given to Lilith, based on the presence of owls. This is the result
of an early mistranslation of a phrase in *Inanna and the Huluppu Tree*,
and neglects the fact that Inanna as goddess of prostitutes was also
seen at dusk, like the *lilu*, hunting for men. The supine lions are
undeniably hers and rest on a scaled plinth that is the convention for
mountains, the realm of the *kur*. Others have suggested the figure is
her sister Ereshkigal, but this is by no means secure. What is certain
is that the horned crown, rod and ring, wings and bird feet appear in
other depictions of Inanna.

The final layer of confusion is added with a psychoanalytical
stratum, notably the work of Barbara Black Koltuv, which though
inspiring to many, is unreliable source material. In this last twist,
the worst aspects of a minor demon become the rejected shadow
of the female psyche. Making cult to a child-killing demon might
make psychological sense, but how much wiser to embrace a goddess
whose powers extend in all eight directions. Witchcraft should take
all the power it can get.

Driven to the shadows, the *rotting goddess,* as styled by Jacob Rabinowitz, has become the demonised ghoul of a witch. The moon
now becomes a street light, the prostitute not standing on behalf of
the goddess, but standing half lit, reviled. It is as if we are only to
celebrate the dark moon mystery and menstruation as curse, never
the opposite. We should for this reason cleave to fifteen. Isis is also
named as the Goddess 15, the number repeats with insistence. Why is

this full moon so important? She is named for her moment of maximum potency. The full moon is the quintessence. She has not been eclipsed into malefica but is in a state of exultation. The full moon is not merely the culmination of the cycle, it is a gate which opens up into a path outside of time.

Kali is another great lady named as the Goddess 15. Kali deserves our attention, but hers is the dark fortnight of the waning moon. This is the time of menstruation, one of withdrawal and seclusion rather than the expansive time of the sabbat and full moon. The waxing moon is more properly Lalita, also entitled the Red Goddess, or if we wish to consider the dyad, glyphed as Varahi and Kurukulla. We have already highlighted some of the vital parallels between Kaula tantra tradition and witchcraft. In many ways we can consider that the yogini is the witch, though in stating this we must be wary of generalisation, the eight petalled lotus is not the eight pointed star. Kali is in a sense, another form of the rotting goddess, for her rites are those of the graveyard, of the black night of Time, and not a plaything for neopagan appropriation. We would do better to consider our own dark moon rites however beguiling the jewels of Mother India. There is another angle to consider: the impact of Mesopotamian civilisation on the Indus Valley and the pre-Aryan goddesses. It is entirely conceivable that Tantra itself bears the very imprint of Inanna. The gate of the dark moon is another aspect of the Goddess 15, which we have seen is the time for preparation of the flying ointment. As our focus has been on the central rite of European witchcraft, namely the sabbat, this has been occluded. Perhaps the best way to signal its importance and very nature is in this absence and deliberate omission. It is the shadow beneath the wings of this text, but enfolded as a blood seed at the heart of the sabbat.

The Goddess 15 has a further secret to impart. The nature of catastrophe which comes upon us as the lunar eclipse. It is a syzygy, sun, earth and moon stand in alignment. Here our symbolic structure seems to disintegrate into a chaos of noise, Ishtar, laughing as the full moon, in opposition to rule, runs red with blood. The harmony of the full moon celebration is plunged into turmoil. This was a phenomenon that the Babylonian astrologers calculated with the Saros cycle and saw as a baleful omen and threat to the king who was replaced by a double for its duration who was then swiftly put to death. They recorded the associated meteorological phenomena of wind, rain, thunder and lightning with the wind direction giving an indication of which of the four lands the disaster would foretell. This ties in to the menstrual mythology, where female blood is the most disruptive and dangerous of magical substances. The raw uncooked blood of the creative matrix extinguishes the fire. No man can be present at this event. Such an action of taboo and seeming caprice is typical of Inanna; she who makes kings can also destroy them. For witchcraft, standing in opposition to a tyrannical order, this is an energy which promises a *coup d'état* and a *coup de foudre*.

How then are we to approach the goddess of witchcraft? Let us emerge from the eclipse bloody, victorious and proclaim the witchcraft anew. The goddess has been with us since the beginning. She is Love and War. This is not paradox, they come from the same erotic juncture. She is centre stage in the battle. Our goddess embodies opposites, and is the quintessence of all that flows through her. Her retinue of demons have joined the carnival. This tumult of goats and satyrs and galli, of mænads and engodded women. Her name has continued to change as it is drawn out of our throats from deep in our bellies, wombs, wounds. Low magic has preserved her rites, as has the litany of our enemies. We are not a reconstruction, we are a reanimation of the bones of ancestry, and they dance.

This is how we encounter her on the sabbat ground. But looking about us, she has in this instant: vanished.

Ted Hughes, in the travails of his despair seeks to write a creation myth. What comes out is *Crow*, the darkest feather dress. *Crow* despoils, murders, pecks away at the raw openings. It is the most harrowing and unsparing of nigredo. The *caput mortuum* does not simply regard him from empty sockets but is strutting, prying, mocking and as with all monsters, indestructible. From this dead head will come the conjuror's trick. Crow has a quest of his own, and goes in search of the black beast. More compelling than Yeats in his gaunt *Second Coming*, Hughes is mired in the natural world, the source of all witchcraft. *Crow* relentlessly asks the question of the poet: *Where is the black beast?* A nightmare unfolds in this vision quest. Finally the reader realises that they are this monster, this beast. With this the dove is revealed and in the same instant sundered, its gorgon blood producing prodigies and chimeras that multiply without end. The secret of witchcraft is written in this myrrh ink.

But let me make this more apparent. The absence of the goddess is the sign of the presence of the witch. She is not external, but is enfleshed. The wild goddess has passed through the city of whoredom and has emerged intact as the witch on the heath. There was never one goddess of witchcraft, but rather a thousand Ishtars: milk white, blood red, lamp black. There can never be orthodoxy. We are simultaneously possessed, annihilated and forever outside of Time.

She is immanent.

She dwells within us.

IX

This the blood cup
Of New Year
Calibrated
Star-tracked
To fatal place
Idin-Dagaz goes
A goat caught
On swastika thorns
Heart drum muffled
By south wind storm
A lapis bead lost
From broken choker
Her priestess
King-making gate
Straddles him
Cedar smooth
Strikes lightning
With thunder roll
Of cunt muscle
Inanna dances down

Hic Rhodus, hic salta!

*... until finally that situation is created which renders all
retreats impossible and conditions themselves cry out:
Hic Rhodus, hic salta! Here is the rose, dance here.*

Still the nature of the art remains elusive. This flux is the very nature of witchcraft, and as such daunting to those who wish to apprehend a method, something which can seem entirely absent. Witchcraft is poetry, not blank prose, even at its most abstract it is underpinned with rhythm, metre, rhyme. It is cyclical. The words themselves carry meaning which has been worn into them, which issues from their split fissures, that fingers out in gentle tendrils, which conceals the undrawn sword of our song. Poetry is not a metaphor, it is the method of witchcraft in its entirety.

The question is not what are the techniques of witchcraft, which are by their nature so simple they can be taught to a child, rather the question is, how do we become a witch? This is harder. In an attempt to achieve this, many turn to supposed authority, but it cannot be easily taught. We do not need to begin with an exterior cult if we can diligently apply the basic exercises, and in doing so nurture the flowering of our own gifts. If we do not have the will to do so, seeking it outside ourselves will not remedy this. Even if we choose to work in congress with supportive others, we will ultimately need to take flight alone. This is the fundamental difference between the witch and the celebrant. We are asked to give more. We are bound by our vows to relinquish everything.

Perhaps, having been schooled that the secrets are truly occult, you need further convincing. Let me offer the example of Jorge Luis Borges, whose poems are too mannered, but whose cut facet prose is a treasury composed of living tigers. In *The Sect of the Phœnix* Borges adumbrates the existence of a body of adepts who conceal a universal secret which is embodied in a rite. I defer to his words:

> The Secret is sacred, but always somewhat ridiculous; its performance is furtive, and even clandestine and the adept do not speak of it. There are no decent words to name it, but it is understood that all words name it...

This brief *cuento* which promises to reveal and never does is the epitome of the game of the magician, who in the tarot is simply a mountebank, fleecing the fool in a cup and ball game. But yet, the secret tantalises us. It cannot be written, but it is always being revealed. The sect exists everywhere and nowhere. This is a game the alchemists played with much enthusiasm, often in poetic exchanges. This elision is an art Debord raises to virtuosity in his autobiography *Panegyric* which reveals precisely nothing. This is a text worth studying as it is a trope much utilised in occult writing, though with far less literary merit. The poets have not been so guarded, as they set out to reveal, rather than portion out such simple matters and in doing so find endless creative expression. This is because the source of poetry and witchcraft are identical, something which Graves understood but could not embody.

Given that the techniques of witchcraft are either simple tricks, or incommunicable to those who do not already understand the secret, it is inevitable that a literature would grow around it with the voracity of thorns which, however well-meaning the sowers were, has nonetheless created an invasive barricade of spines. I cut this down, I harvest these thorns, I make this the haft of my shod stang, and striking the earth clearly proclaim my intent.

I want to avoid the prevalent pyramid schemes by proposing not an order, which I am quite capable of concocting, but a set of three simple principles and interlinked processes which together create a mythic topography of witchcraft which will be entirely yours. When I call this approach apocalyptic witchcraft it is assumed that everything is lost, other than your body, and like a dancer you need to be possessed by it again. Its very simplicity is a ward.

Witchcraft can be seen as an art accomplished through the action of a set of three simple principles, namely: orientation, presence and imperative. These are the three phases which together create a mythic topography of witchcraft. Without these we have only the broken spars of folklore, misreadings of Christian apocrypha, and blind impulse. This is my narrow path into the dark wood.

To begin the process of orientation, we often begin with comparison. This in itself shows the extent to which our own tradition has been broken. We are in the West standing in the wreckage of culture, and without an understanding of our history can make no progress. Modern dazed paganism often makes this mistake, choosing to take the palatable aspects of an imagined past and from them fashion an escape into unrealised fantasy. This has been exacerbated by the collapse of the belief in a European Witch Cult, what can be called the Murray thesis, provoked by both friendly and hostile historians. In order to protect cherished beliefs that have been proved false, we often cling to fantasies, and much of modern pagan witchcraft has found itself in such an impasse. It is in a suspended state of cognitive dissonance, but beginning its arc of entropic decay of locked empty postures and meaningless gestures. Others are more rigorous, this is reconstruction, an approach that might be personally fulfilling, but can only ultimately create a doomed historical anomaly. At its worst, witchcraft in the West is simply *feeling*, a sentimental gush and indulgence that may offer respite to those emotionally wounded by their upbringing, but does not progress beyond this toddler stage. The reflex of this is the canonisation of adolescent emotions, often anger or melancholia, glossed as *primal* or *atavistic,* and a supposed witchcraft that privileges and anchors only those emotional responses. Defining ourselves in opposition to any of these traits leads to internecine squabbling. These must all be understood as honest attempts to find a path, but it is necessary that we propose a constructive alternative to them, one which addresses the deep needs which they mask. We should all engage in critical introspection, this is the mirror for witchcraft to contemplate itself in. Before we begin to apply any kohl we must take a good hard look, not as we are tempted to, at others, but at ourselves.

A search for structure often leads to the cultural appropriation of rites, rituals and symbols from other established traditions, often doing violence to their meaning in the process. Extracted from the cultural framework, these are applied piecemeal. The New Age is one such form of cultural imperialism, and deeply offensive to native peoples. However, the wreckage which we survey in our globalised culture conceals a history rich with significance, and this is the story which this book has told, it is a set of stories which we need to keep repeating. The witch and witchcraft are an historical reality. Yet we quickly come to the conclusion that witchcraft is not the religion that Murray or Gardner proposed, neither is it Durkheim's unified set of beliefs and practices. Perhaps then, there is another way in which we can describe ourselves?

I suggest that witchcraft can best be described as animist, that is, the belief in the all-pervading essence of spirit in all things, whether animals, plants, stones, stars or elements. But this is already problematic, as animism is a term of abuse. It was coined to describe the belief of 'primitive' people and their 'primitive' religion. This distinguished it from the book, chalice, wafer and steel born aloft by their conquerors. It assumed no method, no culture, but a simple set of beliefs erroneously held by the native people whom it considered children. It was not bound into religion (literally *religare*, to bind) and as such could be crushed underfoot with impunity. The practices of tribal people evaded definition in terms of Abrahamic dominator culture, and therefore intelligible meaning. It was simply *magic* and *superstition*, powers that could not match those of acquisition, ownership, disease and systematic genocide by a militarily superior invader. Our fleeting prosperity in the West is built on the stolen blood, labour and soil of Empire. Animism implied a simply personal understanding, and as such was inadequate to explain the complex relationships that underlie the shamanic experience of the multiverse. It did not give credence to the underlying mythic reality of specific people in specific place.

This has been the same fate apportioned to the witch in the West, whose existence was written on water. My thesis is not that we anchor the witch in history, but that we understand that witchcraft is a set of relationships whose rhythm is that of the moon, stars, sun and earth. A witchcraft which adapts to the state of the world as it is, not backing into an imagined past.

Should we then scour our dictionaries for a less loaded term? I suggest we do not. The word *animism* should be raw, as it is a wound that is still being scoured. Like *witch* it has the ambiguity and history that gives it meaning. Should we then be volunteering our data to researchers, digital archives, the State? Must we make ourselves acceptable by aping the conventions of organised religion? Do we need to become part of the lie of a linear progression that tells us history is the successive Ages of metals, that is war, and that this, the bloody end of the brief age of oil which can still end in the reign of uranium, is the pinnacle of our achievement as a species? I say, enough. I say that this beckoning twilight is the space witchcraft is gathering within. Our strength is hydra-headed, rising from the blood of the sacrificially slain dove.

Orientation demands a mythic topography of witchcraft to replace the lost dream of a unified witch cult. Without this element, we are truly lost. The ground upon which we walk is trackless, but the heavens are not. So, rather than a map of the ground, we need a map of the heavens, and this map is the hourglass of time: the moon. In pursuing the work of Shuttle and Redgrove in *The Wise Wound*, a discerning approach to Lévi-Strauss, and through the unapologetic reading of Chris Knight's *Blood Relations*, the myth has been laid before us. This myth has been found in the words of the poets, and in the deeds of the witches' sabbat, night flight and animal transformation. It is under the auspices of both goddess and devil who have been revealed as one. This myth inhabits a landscape.

The elements are simple and not proscriptive. As I describe the landscape, understand that this is a way to enter your own inner world. It is from simple principles that complex behaviours emerge, never the other way around. This bears reading again, the mirror endlessly repeats, reflects, refracts. Let us build our agreement from these simple things, and then let us celebrate our differences as they begin to flourish in their own right and bloom like night jasmine; a scent to steadily slowly inhale. This is the narcotic sensuous landscape which we will find release into by moonlight. The landscape that we are drawn into. The picture that compellingly swells and engorges you into the story. The wordless book, which falls opens and you with it, into the very page. The last flutter, the stilling, the folding in, that merges into the sense of being lifted, the drift. We are both present and utterly gone. Finding ourselves in this new place, our hands look different as we turn them over under the moonlight. This is somewhere to slowly explore, become used to the surroundings beyond the body. Begin to move towards, be moved by the blind magnetic blood. There is a mountain, fairy hill or temple mound. It rises out of the landscape as if it pivots upon the pole star, a vertiginous twisting. A spiralling motion that spins transfixed and never loses its balance. The moon climbs this hill and descends the other side. Tonight it is full. Within the hill there is a cave, there has always been a cave. This cave is the broiling cauldron of the Underworld. Within the cave, the dark, within the dark, the sun, animating the memory locked in the stacked bones of ancestors. This is the axis mundi. Let the image bloom like the night jasmine we are inhaling, let the eyes find their place of rest. Remember that you have been here before, barefoot, wolf-shod. The moon weeps while you dance. The cup slowly fills to the brim, drop by precious drop. Your feet have found the steps to the sabbat and so must dance, dance, dance.

This bears reading again before sleep, the mirror endlessly repeats, reflects, refracts. Our inner orientation is the result of this dreaming. The moon caught within the sleeping body of the witch, as if in a mirror. We must know these, our secret interiors and explore them ourselves before we invite others to explore them with us. Coven forms around the shared dream built from these journeys. Everyone is equal in this naked state; is strong, wholly true and royal. The body of the sabbat forms as more are drawn by the vortex. We all share the same ground, simply dream differently. All are ultimately pooled in the ritual consanguinity of animal, woman, witch, spirit, devil, ancestor, and man.

This orientation becomes more complex, as our vision is constellated through the process of communion. We become attuned to the lunar rhythms, but as with the antler batons of our ancestors, soon these become inscribed with other animal forms which too mark time. As we find others, their symbols become part of our dream landscape. Perhaps we choose to move through the landscape with the solar year as well as the thirteen moons. Perhaps spirits begin to ask that we pay heed to them. All this is a matter of free choice. It arises from the dreaming body which has liberated itself from undue influence, from parasite. The dreaming of the witch is not built, it is trodden. Cult can be the result of these actions, but it is not their origin.

The second principle of an apocalyptic witchcraft is Presence. The witch, unlike the gnostic, does not make a fatal and inimical division between spirit and flesh. One paradox of the sabbat is that the night flight is achieved through and in the flesh itself. This is where the motif of the wounded wolf once more lifts up its bandaged paw to make us bear witness. A silent understanding is exchanged. This is the essence of animism, not as an approach, but as a lived existence. The witch must be present, and this presence means the body. We must learn to stand within ourselves, to achieve the equilibrium, the fixity of the witch's nail. Before we are able to leap as marionettes, hung from the heavens, we must know that we have grown from the earth. Our state is one of cultivated in-betweeness. We are neither one, nor the other, but going from state to state in endless fluid transformation. We are able to mediate, precisely because we are other. We are justice, poised in order that we can freely move in any chaotic direction.

Further, we are impelled by the heavens to, like the dancer, extend beyond the very tips of our extension. Like the martial artist trains, we are not to punch at, but through. We must find the limits of our endurance and stretch them further. Presence is not given, it is attained, not retained, but endlessly strived for. We are as much a bow to be drawn as the moon itself. The arrow seeks its mark.

Our aim is to become as receptive as the moon, in order that we can contain all the reflected solar fire and pour it out as libation, or curses. We listen. We observe. We absorb. We master silence and stillness, stealth. We are able to become ceaseless and undiminished in our giving. It is we who light, tend and extinguish the hearth fires. Fire flows through us and it is we who endure.

Presence is in the refinement of the senses. Their calibration achieved through an orientation that becomes embodied. This encompasses the gestalt of all five senses. We must train our limbs, organs, tendons, muscles and lock this learning into our bones. Otherwise we are degenerate animals, clinging mournfully to our sickness and ill couched in lassitude. We will not accept the victim body, just as we will not accept the victim culture. We have the eyes of owls, the tread of cats, the mourning song of wolves, and the mastery of lions. The witch is integrated, and moves unselfconsciously, like the animals she is intimate with. Witchcraft nurtures strength, and from this body issues speech and action.

We follow the cycles in the heavens, in our bodies, and then the spirit comes through us. This is the secret of possession; it manifests where we stand. Without presence, there can be no possession, only obsession spasming through a cluttered social body. Such a vessel will only rupture as it seeks to break through its confining carapace. This is all too often the case. Witchcraft is a body of work.

Standing present within ourselves requires that we know the ground we are standing on. This has been not so much the great failure of witchcraft, but the great victory of our age. The world has been cut from beneath our very feet. We no longer know where we are: Tokyo, Paris, Baghdad blur beneath the demands of another imposed architecture of manufactured dreams. Our surroundings are replaced with their wraiths, in a gnostic parable gone awry. Yet the world is not a rotten place, or black iron prison for the witch. We should not be so susceptible to accepting an overghosting of our mental territory and the diminuition of the world itself. If we have found our inner orientation, we can count ourselves free, or at least engaged in the struggle for this freedom. By glibly accepting the orientation of our culture we are not engaged with the mythic, but with the banal. This has consequences; the greatest of these is Nature herself.

Witchcraft has not stood up. It has inhaled the warm fumes of fantasy, lost in so many different dreams. Forgotten perhaps, what it was once for. It is presence which is called for. Here we must state the clear difference between witchcraft and so-called esotericism: it is contained in that derided term, animism. In witchcraft there is no separation between the spiritual and the material, they are inter-penetrated. We are not seeking to escape, but to encounter. This is glyphed in the union at the heart of the sabbat, not only between the queen and her consort, but in the flesh of all those present. This is the sheer truth which Ted Hughes realised, wrote out, that Peter Redgrove felt in the electrical play of storm clouds building in the weather factory of the Fal Estuary in Kernow, whose discharge makes the black mud sing. It is out there in the hills, forests and mountains, it is pounding in our chests, lifting, swelling, puckering, running wet in our mutable flesh. This is the witchcraft, and it is the secret face of nature herself. Nature veiled not with the dawn dew cobwebs, the high cloud that hangs above the peak, the churned opal of surf, but by our own incomprehension. The natural world is the supernatural world of witchcraft, shot through with the vivid silks of sunset and sunrise. Shadows burned to nothing by the midday sun, midnight's pallor thrown on old stones. What foolishness it is to not realise that this is the landscape upon which our dreams are founded.

The mythic is not an overlay, it is the worn cupolas in the rock quoits stacked on the barren moors. It is the black earth of the barrows. The earth is pregnant with meaning, with tumuli and foreboding entrances slanting down into the underworld which we have crawled from on skinned knees into solstice morning dawns. This is magic, this is what demands our presence, and furthermore, this is what is at stake.

This leads to the final proposition of the entire thesis, the third and final phase, and the most critically difficult of them all. We would like to put up barriers against the truth that we are all one flesh. We need ritual strategies to overcome our internal resistance to this absolute tangible reality of witchcraft. It drives us to the liminal spaces where the witchcraft can get through, where we are part of the warp and weft, weaving on the fatal loom. Our heads are for the most part severed from the season's suffering birth. Our lives absent of meaning, of even celestial time, we mistake watching for doing and another's reflection for our own. How much easier if we never grasp this central aching truth. How much more preferable would be the sheer fantasia of disembodied spirit, ignoring the mortal demands, the messages and omens that are Cassandra's gift. So we drift on soothing murmurs as caged doves, numbed by dreams that never reveal the divine as serpent, light, love. But the witch, sleeping with one eye open, stares into the secret.

Seeing ourselves in dream requires that we see ourselves in life, in specific place and at specific time. The mirror must be our own true reflection. This is not an escape, we have been hunted down, buckling exhausted before the wolf-ankled huntress. Having undressed ourselves, the ultimate mirror is shown to be nature herself. We inhabit the sacred landscape which is the form of the body of witchcraft and the witch, with the embodied knowledge that her fate is inseparable from ours. It cannot be outrun. The rivers are our veins, the trees our lungs, the water our blood, the stones our bones, the earth our flesh, the winds our breath, the storm our anger. This is not as metaphor, but lived, trodden into us. Above this the moon ceaselessly pours out her life, and is endlessly fed on offerings of semen and blood.

We have reached the irrepressible and sexual core of all witchcraft practice. An apocalyptic witchcraft needs a revelation, and here is mine, stated with simplicity as all witchcraft should be. After orientation and presence there can only be one outcome. A third principle flowers, though when we reach for it, when the scent has thralled us, the petals beguiled us into their labyrinth, life jolts startled from a pricked finger. The whole rose garden comes into focus. We are awake. The third principle is: Imperative. The blood tastes of copper, the green moss of verdigris that spreads and webs the living metal, the goddess whose endless war shrikes us all. The knowledge of death cascades through us. With this, the curse is given.

This poison, this death, gifts you the imperative. Talk of nature is not a soft mossy bank, nor a wandervogel idealism. It has a totenkopf reply, in raven's feathers, carnival mask, pearls. To have come this far, you knew what the answer of the oracle would be, croaking out from a throat sore from laughter. Death, death, death. Robert Graves saw death in the shaving mirror, scowling at its mask of age: 'He still stands ready, with a boys presumption, To court the queen in her high silk pavilion.' He claws after young girls with bony fingers, unable to move on. We must live with passion, but death is our field of action, without which there can be no life. We can never be prepared for this unless we keep dying on the Sabbat ground with all the rouged beauty of samurai. We surrender, we let go of everything. We let her act through us until we have nothing to lose.

Witchcraft is defined in that it acts. This is not a path of contemplation, but of engagement. There can be only one reason to engage, and that is that the action is imperative. Witchcraft grew from need. In shamanic culture the role is very clear. The shaman is expected to deal with issues of life and death on a daily basis. Hunger is a reality, starvation, war, disease, cursing, theft, murder, childbirth, hunting.

For us, huddled in the narrow apse of the technological age, these concerns seem remote. Each of these skills has been prised from us. The shaman must act because the stakes are high, it is survival, life that hangs in the balance. He is expected by his community to produce results, or be considered worthless. His night flights have purpose, his cures and curses are in demand. His reading of omens, his telling of story, his organising of the hunt or war, are vital. Compare this to the state of the West. Our ritual specialists do not have to demonstrate any competence or effect. There is no *need* but simply *want*. With nothing to play for, with no stakes on the table, the game inevitably becomes an empty charade.

So what is the imperative of apocalyptic witchcraft? What prevents it being another glass bead game to vainly attempt to cheat death of her prize, but merely deludes the player by absolving them of all responsibility for their petty actions? The answer has already been given, and it is animism. Witchcraft is part of a living web of species and relationships, a world which we have forgotten to observe, understand or inhabit. Many people reading this paragraph will not know even the current phase of the moon, and if asked for it will not instinctively look up to the correct quarter of the sky, but down to their computers. Neither will they be able to name the plants, birds or animals within a metre or a mile radius of their door. Witchcraft asks that we do these first things, this is presence.

Animism is not embedded in the natural world, it *is* the natural world. Our witchcraft is that of spirit of place, which is made from a convergence of elements and inhabitants. Here I include animals, both living and dead, human and inhuman. Our helpers are mammals, reptiles, fish, birds and insects. Some can be counted allies, others are more ambivalent. Predator and prey are interdependent. These all have the same origin and ancestry, they come from plants, from copper green life. Bones become soil. The plants have been nourished on the minerals drawn up from the bowels of the earth. These are the living tools of the witch's craft. The cycle of the elements and seasons is read in this way. Flux, life and death are part of

163

this, as are extinctions, catastrophe, fire and flood. We avail ourselves of these, and ultimately a balance is sought. Our ritual space is written in starlight, watched over by sun and moon.

So this leaves us with a simple question. How can there be any Witchcraft if this is destroyed? It is not a rhetorical question. Our land, our trees, animals and elements hold spirit. Will we let our familiars, literally our family be destroyed? If we have any real belief and experience of spirit, then it does not ask, it demands us to fight for it.

Our civilisation is not one of life. It is not the lioness muzzling the breath from a gazelle, nor the striving of a virus, nor the honesty of a bronze blade. It has no sense or awareness, no presence and no orientation.

I have heard it said that a land wight does not care about the politics of who summons it. This is a glib statement. It is politics which enables the destruction of the very land which the wight stands guard over. Man is a political animal, those who say that they are outside of, or above, politics are the esotericists whose clean hands are washed in the blood of those who have no choice but to put their hands in the machinery. Politics is not optional for First Nations, women, homosexuals, blacks, or any of the other slave classes. Abstention is a position of privilege which aids the pattern of destruction, arguing only for our impotence. There is no left-right dichotomy, there are those who are destroying the body, and those who stand against them. Economics is war by other means, and in this asymmetric war against life itself, you do not have the luxury of choice. This is the time when our witchcraft again becomes an imperative, or perishes.

Witchcraft cannot come in any colour other than a deep green, a resistance to this despoilment, this sacrilege. Picking up litter at our ritual sites makes no difference when our world is a landfill of broken consumer dreams. Calling the quarters oblivious that the water table has fallen and the sea levels are rising, firestorms sweep Australia and Brazil, our soil which takes a thousand years to grow an inch has blown away, is mindless indulgence. Animism cannot disengage from the struggle of life, shamanism cannot disengage from the struggle of life, neither can a living witchcraft. No-one else is going to do this for us. We are the Witchcraft and must stand for our land, and with those who fight for their own.

It is only when nothing is considered sacred that this destruction is able to occur. The origins of androcentrism are written into Genesis as a dominator meme, the script runs thus: *everything belongs to us and for us, amen*. It is a rapist's charter. Christianity has been laid aside, the justifications have changed, but the mechanism remains flexing its iron jaws. Jahweh is now the market piggybacking on industrial civilisation, the tools it has are more than bronze axes, its appetites insatiable, rare earths, metals, oils, gas, animals, fish, birds, plants, cattle, men. John Michael Greer highlights the logical fallacy of infinite growth on a finite planet, but this is the slogan of those who will cut down your last trees, poison your last wells and slaughter your people. It is a continuation of the actions we find enshrined in Isaiah. We may be called perverse for our beliefs, but this is an obscenity. We must engage in deliberate enchantment, draw the line which cannot be crossed. Our land, our ancestors, our bodies, our blood and our kin are inviolable. Our enemies can be slain.

The examples I have given of landscape throughout, are my own, not those of an imagined rural idyll. My known nature is red in tooth and claw. This is why I respond to the poetry of Ted Hughes, understand Redgrove's obsession with water as it scours the granite and slate of the land of my birth. I bear reef scars and coral cuts, my calves are corded from walking in woods and hills, I prefer to be amongst mountains than men, and know that this, my birth right, is now a privilege. So I state, there is no escape or withdrawal possible, we have our backs against the furthest wall of the cave and the shapes of animals bulge against us, pressing us forward. Ted Kaczynski found this to his cost. I make no apology to those in the cities, nor do I doubt the efficacy of magic performed in the world of Lyre. As the oligarchs dispossess us of our land, as the sprawl edges out on every last drop of dirty oil and pulverised slaggish coke, more of us will be engulfed. What I say is vital: the urban environment cannot exist without murdering the natural world. We must then be the wilderness in the heart of the city. As civilisation pushes into the wilderness, some will stand in its path, others will already be inside, besieging its towers in the twilight. The devil will open the locks for us. None shall stand before Her.

Despair haunts those who know the cost being exacted from the earth. They are driven by pain, rage and despair, they hurt. We have a duty to them, and all those who suffer, drawing no distinction between spirit, animal, plant, stone or man. What drives us is our blood, the passions and emotions are our power which makes it sing with fire. Like the land, these passions are not owned by individuals, but are subsumed in Love, shared in communion; we are the daughters and sons of comfort. Life itself is at stake in not some longed-for apocalypse which opens into a Golden Age, but the betrayal of our ancestors and our duty of care, of balance. We will not watch as the final price is exacted in the blood of all living things. Without action, these will be the last hundred years, not just of man, but of all life.

Witchcraft is inoculated against despair with poison, our bones given over, our blood promised. We who are already dead will baptise our children in the name of the witchcraft. Our sabbats will grow. The witch will not lie still in the ground. This is why we are burned, liberated, that we may not walk with our vengeance, nor rise on Judgement Day. But the moon rises, red with the blood that endlessly replenishes the cup. We are present, manifest in flesh and dream. We return, with the vengeance of love singing through our veins.

So we circle round at last to the epigram: *Hic rhodus, hic salta!* I have chosen the phrase because it encapsulates both the imperative for action and the whole truth of witchcraft. My meaning is neither that of Marx nor Hegel nor Æsop from whom the phrase and its subsequent misunderstanding came. I like that the Latin is simple, carved and sparce, yet there is space in it for us to find our own reading. It is brief enough to be inscribed in a simple locket, short enough to be memorised and turned around by the tongue. Like witchcraft, and those who practice it, the epigram offers no apologies for itself, it simply is. There are no religious trappings, no named divinity, no allegiance to Crown, State or personage. It is as clear as spring well water. It is the motto for apocalyptic witchcraft in that it needs no support, just the body of the witch through whom the meaning will flower. It throws down a deliberate challenge. The words read thus:

Here is the rose,
Dance here.

x

Whore star of heaven
Innana ascends on song
A skirl of petticoats
Sweetly reveals her youth
Tender as an axe head
Smashed pomegranate wise
She gifts us this
Love

Bibliography

APOCALYPTIC WITCHCRAFT/MANIFESTO

DIMECH, ALKISTIS, *Coup de Foudre* in *XVI*. Scarlet Imprint, 2010.

FEDERICI, SILVIA, *Caliban and the Witch: Women, the Body and Primitive Accumulation*. Autonomedia, 2004.

GREY, PETER, *Seeing through Apocalypse* in *XVI*. Scarlet Imprint, 2010.

HUSON, PAUL, *Mastering Witchcraft*. G.P. Putnam's Sons, New York, 1970.

HOWARD, MICHAEL, *Children of Cain: A Study of Modern Traditional Witches*. Three Hands Press, 2011.

HUTTON, RONALD, *The Triumph of the Moon*. Oxford, 1999.

MICHELET, JULES, *Satanism and Witchcraft*, (trans. by A.R. ALLINSON). The Citadel Press, New York, 1946.

PARSONS, JOHN WHITESIDE, *Freedom is a Two-Edged Sword*. Falcon Press, 1989.

SENECA, LUCIUS ANNÆUS, *Medea* in *Vol. VIII: Tragedies*. Loeb, 1917.

SPRENGER, JACOBUS AND KRAMER, HEINRICH, *Malleus Maleficarum*, The Folio Society, 1968.

SUMMERS, MONTAGUE, *Witchcraft and Black Magic*. Arrow, 1964.

APULEIUS, *The Golden Ass,* Penguin Classics, 1999.

HARRISON, JANE ELLEN, *A Prologomena to the Study of Greek Religion.* Cambridge University Press, 1908.

KINGSLEY, PETER, *In the Dark Places of Wisdom.* The Golden Sufi Center, 1999.

MACDERMOT, VIOLET, *The Cult of the Seer in the Ancient Middle East.* Wellcome Institute of the History of Medicine, London, 1971.

MEIER, C.A., *Healing Dream and Ritual, Ancient Incubation and Modern Psychotherapy.* Daimon Verlag, 1989, 2009.

O'FLAHERTY, WENDY DONIGER, *Dreams, Illusion and Other Realities.* The University of Chicago Press, 1984.

ROBERTS, NEIL, *A Lucid Dreamer: The Life of Peter Redgrove.* Jonathan Cape, 2012.

PACHE, CORINNE ONDINE, *A Moment's Ornament: The Poetics of Nympholepsy in Ancient Greece.* Oxford University Press, 2011.

PLATO, *Phædrus,* Penguin Classics, 2005.

RYAN, ROBERT E., *The Strong Eye of Shamanism.* Inner Traditions, 1999.

SPARE, AUSTIN OSMAN, *Ethos.* IHO, 2001.

STRATTON-KENT, JAKE, *Geosophia: The Argo of Magic, Vols. 1 & 2.* Scarlet Imprint, 2010.

USTINOVA, YULIA, *Caves and the Ancient Greek Mind.* Oxford, 2009.

WILSON, PETER LAMBORN, *"Shower of Stars" Dream and Book: The Initiatic Dream in Sufism and Taoism.* Autonomedia, 1996.

A SPELL TO AWAKEN ENGLAND

Opening quote from HUGHES, TED, *Winter Pollen.* Faber & Faber, 1994.

GRAVES, ROBERT, *The White Goddess.* Carcanet, 1997.

HUGHES, TED, *Collected Poems* (edited by PAUL KEEGAN). Faber and Faber, 2003.

———, *Letters of Ted Hughes* (Selected & edited by CHRISTOPHER REID). Faber and Faber, 2007.

———, *Tales from Ovid.* Farar, Straus, Giroux, 1997.

———, *Shakespeare and the Goddess of Complete Being.* Faber and Faber, 1992.

REDGROVE, PETER, *Collected Poems* (edited by NEIL ROBERTS). Jonathan Cape, 2012.

———, *The Black Goddess and the Sixth Sense*. Bloomsbury, 1987.

SAGAR, KEITH, *The Laughter of Foxes: A study of Ted Hughes*. Liverpool University Press, 2000.

———, *The Art of Ted Hughes*. Cambridge University Press, 1975.

SHUTTLE, PENELOPE & REDGROVE, PETER, *The Wise Wound*. Marion Boyars, 2005.

SKEA, ANN, *Ted Hughes: The Poetic Quest*. The University of New England Press, 1994.

THE SCAFFOLD OF LIGHTNING

BURNETT, CHARLES, *Magic and Divination in the Middle Ages*. Variorum, 1996.

HUSON, PAUL, *The Devil's Picture Book*. Abacus, 1972.

KERÉNYI, CARL, *Dionysos, Archetypal Image of Indestructible Life*. Princeton University Press, 1976.

OTTO, WALTER F., *Dionysus, Myth and Cult* (trans. by R. B. PALMER). Indiana University Press, 1965.

PÓCS, ÉVA, *Between the Living and the Dead*. Central European University Press, 1999.

REDGROVE, PETER, *The God of Glass*. Routledge & Kegan Paul, 1979.

———, *The Sleep of the Great Hypnotist: the life and death and life after death of a modern magician*. Routledge & Kegan Paul, 1979.

———, *The Facilitators, or Mister Hole-in-the-Day*. Routledge & Kegan Paul, 1982.

TYSON, DONALD, *The Demonology of James I*. Llewellyn, 2011.

WILBY, EMMA, *Cunning Folk & Familiar Spirits: Shamanistic Visionary Traditions in Early Modern British Witchcraft and Magic*. Sussex Academic Press, 2005.

———, *The Visions of Isobel Gowdie – Magic, Witchcraft and Dark Shamanism in Seventeenth-Century Scotland*. Sussex Academic Press, 2010.

THE CHILDREN THAT ARE HIDDEN AWAY

Opening quote from BLAKE, WILLIAM, *The Garden of Love* from. *Songs of Experience, 1794.*

ABUSCH, I. TZVI & VAN DER TOORN, K. (EDS.), *Mesopotamian Magic: Textual, Historical, & Interpretative Perspectives.* Styx, 1999.
CIXOUS, HÉLÈNE & CLÉMENT, CATHERINE, *The Newly Born Woman,* (translated by BETSY WING). Manchester University Press, 1987.
CIXOUS, HÉLÈNE, 'The Laugh of the Medusa.' (trans. KEITH COHEN, PAULA COHEN), in *Signs* 1, No. 4 1976. The University of Chicago Press.
GAGNÉ, RENAUD, *Winds and Ancestors: The Physika of Orpheus* in *Harvard Studies in Classical Philology, Vol. 103.* Harvard University, 2007.
GINZBURG, CARLO, *The Night Battles.* Johns Hopkins, 1992.
———, *Ecstasies: Deciphering the Witches' Sabbath.* Hutchinson Radius, 1990.
KNIGHT, CHRIS, *Blood Relations: The Menstrual Origins of Culture.* Yale University Press, 1991.
RÄTSCH, CHRISTIAN, *The Encyclopedia of Psychactive Plants.* Park Street Press, 2005.
ROHDE, ERWIN, *Psyche: The Cult of Souls and Belief in Immortality among the Greeks.* Kegan Paul, 1925.
WELSFORD, ENID, *The Court Masque: A Study in the Relationship Between Poetry & the Revels.* Cambridge University Press, 1927.
WHITE, DAVID GORDON, *Kiss of the Yogini, "Tantric Sex" in its South Asian Contexts.* University of Chicago Press, 2003.

A WOLF SENT FORTH TO SNATCH AWAY A LAMB

ALBRIGHT, W. F., *The Goddess of Life and Wisdom,* from The American Journal of Semitic Languages & Literatures, Vol. 36, No. 4, July 1920.
BARING-GOULD, SABINE, *The Book of Werewolves.* London, 1865.
JARRY, ALFRED, *Messalina.* Atlas, 1985.
LÉVI-STRAUSS, CLAUDE, *The Raw and the Cooked.* Chicago University Press, 1983.
MISHEV, GEOGI, *Thracian Magic.* Avalonia, 2012.
OGIER, DARRYL, *Night Revels and Werewolfery in Calvinist Guernsey,* in Folklore, Vol. 109, 1998.

SENN, HARRY, *Romanian Werewolves: Seasons, Ritual, Cycles* in Folklore, Vol. 93, No. 2, 1982.

DA SILVA, FRANCISCO VAZ, *Iberian Seventh-Born Children, Werewolves, and the Dragon Slayer: A Case Study in the Comparative Interpretation of Symbolic Praxis and Fairytales* in Folklore, Vol. 114, No. 3, Dec., 2003.

STOPHLET FLATTERY, DAVID & SCHWARTZ, MARTIN, *Haoma and Harmaline.* University of California Press, 1989.

TAVERNER, EUGENE, *Studies in Magic from Latin Literature.* Columbia University Press, 1916.

USTINOVA, YULIA, *Lycanthropy in Sarmatian Warrior Societies: the Kobyakovo Torque*, in Ancient West & East, Vol. I, no. 1. Brill, 2002.

FIFTEEN

Opening quote from LE CENCI HAMILTON, LEONIDAS (trans.), *Ishtar and Izdubar.* 1884.

ASTOUR, MICHAEL C., *Hellenosemitica: An Ethnic and Cultural Study in West Semitic Impact on Mycenaean Greece.* Brill, Leiden, 1967.

BARTON, GEORGE A., *The Semitic Ištar Cult* in Hebraica, Vol. 9, No. 3/4 Apr.–Jul., 1893 & Vol. 10, No. 1/2 Oct., 1893 – Jan., 1894.

———, *Tiamat* in Journal of the American Oriental Society, Vol. 15, 1893.

BRUSCHWEILLER, FRANÇOISE, *Inanna: La déesse triomphante et vaincue dans la cosmologie Sumérienne.* Editions Peeters, Leuven, 1987.

CAMPION, NICHOLAS, *A History of Western Astrology: Volume 1, the Ancient World.* Continuum, 2008.

ESHLEMAN, CLAYTON, *Juniper Fuse: Upper Paleolithic Imagination & the Construction of the Underworld.* Wesleyan University Press, 2003.

FONTENROSE, JOSEPH, *Python: A Study of Delphic Myth and its Origins.* University of California Press, 1959.

FROTHINGHAM, A. L., *Medusa, Apollo, and the Great Mother* in American Journal of Archæology, Vol. 15, No. 3, Jul. – Sep., 1911.

GIMBUTAS, MARIA, *The Language of the Goddess.* Thames & Hudson, London, 1989.

———, *The Living Goddesses* (edited & supplemented by DEXTER, M.R.). University of California Press, 1999.

GOFF, BEATRICE, *Symbols of Prehistoric Mesopotamia*. Yale University Press, 1963.

GRAVES, RICHARD PERCEVAL, *Robert Graves and the White Goddess 1940–1985*. Weidenfeld and Nicolson, 1995

LANGDON, S., *Ishtar: A Monograph upon Babylonian Religion & Theology Containing Extensive Extracts from the Tammuz Liturgies & all of the Arbela Oracles*. The Clarendon Press, Oxford, 1914.

MARSHACK, ALEXANDER, *The Roots of Civilization: The Cognitive Beginnings of Man's First Art, Symbol and Notation*. McGraw-Hill, 1972.

MASSEY, GERALD, *The Natural Genesis, Vols. 1 & 2*. Williams & Norgate, 1883.

———, *Luniolatry: Ancient & Modern* in *Gerald Massey's Lectures*. Circa, 1900.

RABINOWITZ, JACOB, *The Rotting Goddess: The Origin of the Witch in Classical Antiquity's Demonization of Fertility Religion*. Autonomedia, 1998.

REED, ELIZABETH A., *Persian Literature, Ancient and Modern*. S. C. Griggs, Chicago, 1893.

RIDDLE, JOHN M., *Eve's Herbs: A History of Contraception and Abortion in the West*. Harvard University Press, 1997.

SCHULKE, D.A., *Veneficium: Magic, Witchcraft and the Poison Path*. Three Hands Press, 2012.

WEST, DAVID REID, *Some cults of Greek goddesses and female dæmons of oriental origin: especially in relation to the mythology of goddesses and demons in the Semitic world*. PhD thesis (1990), University of Glasgow.

WEST, M.L., *The East Face of Helicon*. Clarendon Press, Oxford, 1997.

WHITE, GAVIN, *Babylonian Star-Lore*. Solaria, 2008.

HIC RHODUS, HIC SALTA!

Opening quote from MARX, KARL, *The Eighteenth Brumaire of Louis Bonaparte*. 1852.

ASTOUR, MICHAEL, C., *Tamar the Hierodule: An Essay in the Method of Vestigial Motifs* in Journal of Biblical Literature, Vol. 85, No. 2 (Jun., 1966), pp. 185–196.

BORGES, JORGE, LUIS, *Labyrinths*. Penguin Books, 1970.

DEBORD, GUY, *Panegyric*. Verso, 2004.

DIMECH, ALKISTIS, *Outside the Temple* in *Devoted* (Eds. DIMECH, A. & GREY, P.). Scarlet Imprint, 2008.

GREER, JOHN MICHAEL, *The Blood of the Earth: An Essay on Magic and Peak Oil.* Scarlet Imprint, 2012.

GREY, PETER, *The Amfortas Wound* in *Devoted* (Eds. DIMECH, A. & GREY, P.). Scarlet Imprint, 2008.

JENSON, D., MCBAY, A. & KEITH L., *Deep Green Resistance*. Seven Stories Press, 2011.

RIPINSKY-NAXON, MICHAEL, *The Nature of Shamanism*. State University of New York Press, 1993.

Index